AUDREY
HEPBURN

IN THE MOVIES

AUDREY HEPBURN

IN THE MOVIES

A RETROSPECTIVE BY TIMOTHY KNIGHT

METRO BOOKS

NEW YORK

DESIGNER: Les Krantz with Julie Nor
CONTRIBUTING WRITERS:
Ken DuBois, Michael Fox, Pam Grady, Dennis Kwiatkowski, Sheila Lane,
Debra Ott, James Plath, Tim Sika and Christopher Varaste
COPY EDITOR: Katherine Hinkebein
PHOTO EDITOR: Debbi Andrews
DVD DOCUMENTARY:
Les Krantz (Executive Producer), Jack Piantino (Video Editor)
Kristie Back (Musical Selections)

PHOTO CREDITS:
Everett Collection (pages 12-13, 62-64, 164-166)
Photofest (pages 14-15)

METRO BOOKS
122 Fifth Avenue
New York, NY 10011

ISBN-13: 978-1-4351-1854-6

Library of Congress data available on request

Printed and bound in China by PWGS

1 3 5 7 9 10 8 6 4 2

DEDICATION

For my parents,
William and Mary Ann Knight

ACKNOWLEDGMENTS

I received invaluable advice and assistance from many people while working on this book/documentary package. First and foremost, I am especially grateful to Les Krantz, my mentor and frequent collaborator, whose persistence and vision made *Audrey Hepburn in the Movies* possible. Thanks also to copy editor Katherine Hinkebein, designer Julie Nor and photo editor Debbi Andrews for their exemplary work. Kudos to Jack Piantino and Kristie Back for skillfully assembling and editing the accompanying documentary, and to Jeff Joseph of Sabucat Productions for providing the footage. Finally, my sincere thanks to everyone at Barnes & Noble for their good judgment and staunch support; I am especially indebted to Cynthia Barrett, Mark Levine and Peter Norton.

It was my great good fortune to work with a crackerjack team of writers on *Audrey Hepburn in the Movies*. I cannot thank them enough for their sterling contributions and prodigious work ethic. I tip my hat in gratitude to Ken Dubois, Michael Fox, Pam Grady, Dennis Kwiatkowski, Sheila Lane, Debra Ott, James Plath, Tim Sika and Christopher Varaste.

Scores of online and print sources were checked and cross-checked in the researching and writing of *Audrey Hepburn in the Movies*. Aside from the websites imdb.com, tcm.com and rottentomatoes.com, the *New York Times* online archive and the Academy Awards database, the following books provided the bulk of the information on Hepburn's life and career: *Audrey: Her Real Story* by Alexander Walker (St. Martin's Press, 1994); *Audrey Hepburn* by Barry Paris (Putnam Adult, 1996); *Audrey Hepburn, An Elegant Spirit: A Son Remembers,* by Sean Hepburn Ferrer (Atria, 2005); *The Audrey Hepburn Treasures* by Ellen Erwin and Jessica Z. Diamond (Atria, 2006); and *Enchantment: The Life of Audrey Hepburn* by Donald Spoto (Harmony, 2006).

TABLE OF CONTENTS

INTRODUCTION

When Donald O'Connor announced her name at the 26th Annual Academy Awards on March 25, 1954, Audrey Hepburn strode toward the stage with a quiet dignity rarely seen in a 25-year-old actress, let alone a newcomer who had just won Hollywood's most coveted prize for her first starring role. Then again, there was never anything remotely ordinary or typical about Hepburn, the elegant sylphlike beauty with an incandescent smile that could light up the continental United States.

In the 56 years since *Roman Holiday* transformed the ex-ballerina into a superstar, Audrey Hepburn has inspired the kind of mass adoration usually reserved for deities. If anything, the cult of Hepburn has grown exponentially since her death in 1993. She is probably Hollywood's most *beloved* star, revered for her humanitarian work as well has her film career and innate style. By all accounts modest and self-effacing, Hepburn never bought into her own myth. There are no stories of divalike histrionics or drunken benders in the scores of books, articles and Internet fan

HEPBURN'S GREATEST PERFORMANCES

PRINCESS ANN
Roman Holiday (1953)

Hepburn was crowned Hollywood royalty for her beguiling performance as the runaway princess in search of a *Roman Holiday* (1953). Both director William Wyler and co-star Gregory Peck were entranced by the Belgian-born actress, who had charmed Broadway audiences in *Gigi*. In addition to winning the Academy Award for *Roman Holiday*, Hepburn made the cover of *TIME* and became the darling of the fashion world for her simple yet elegant style.

SABRINA FAIRCHILD
Sabrina (1954)

Hepburn beat the sophomore curse with *Sabrina* (1954), her highly anticipated follow-up to *Roman Holiday*. She received the second of her five Academy Award nominations for her captivating performance as the title character: a chauffeur's daughter transformed into a chic society beauty. Co-starring Humphrey Bogart and William Holden as wealthy brothers vying for Hepburn's Cinderella-like heroine, *Sabrina* earned Hepburn a Golden Globe and confirmed her standing on Hollywood's A-list.

SISTER LUKE
The Nun's Story (1959)

Scrubbed of glamour, Hepburn foregoes Givenchy designs to don a nun's habit in Fred Zinnemann's superb adaptation of Kathryn Hulme's novel. As Gabrielle van der Mal, a devout yet headstrong young woman who enters a Belgian order in the 1920s, Hepburn gives an exquisitely modulated performance that forever silenced critics who had previously doubted her acting ability. Hepburn received her third Academy Award nomination for *The Nun's Story* (1959), which co-stars some of the screen's greatest character actresses: Dame Peggy Ashcroft, Mildred Dunnock, Dame Edith Evans and Beatrice Straight.

sites that exhaustively chronicle her life and career. In the rarefied and pampered world of Hollywood, where every whim is indulged and bad behavior excused as "artistic temperament," Hepburn was a gracious anomaly. This is not to say that she was a saint (although many fans hold her in such regard). She had affairs with co-stars and had a cinematographer fired for failing to shoot her in a flattering light. But except for her *Sabrina* co-star Humphrey Bogart, almost everyone who ever knew or worked with Hepburn spoke of her only in the most glowing terms. As Elizabeth Taylor so movingly put it after Hepburn succumbed to cancer at the age of 62, "God has a most beautiful new angel now that will know just what to do in heaven."

Granted, Hepburn didn't inspire every film critic to wax rhapsodic about her dramatic abilities. In the 1950s, a few critics rashly dismissed her as more of a model than a bona-fide actress. And while Hepburn may not be a screen chameleon like Meryl Streep, or classically trained like Vanessa Redgrave, she is nonetheless an instinctively gifted actress of great delicacy and heartbreaking vulnerability. Above all, she is a star of peerless radiance and irresistible charm that sets her apart from every actress in Hollywood history. Simply put, Hepburn is *sui generis*: a singular talent whose essence cannot be duplicated, no matter how many actresses try to evoke her. Like director and fervent Hepburn admirer Billy Wilder said, "That dress by Mr. Givenchy has already been filled."

Audrey Hepburn in the Movies is a celebration of this extraordinary star who occupies a unique place in the hearts and minds of moviegoers worldwide. Enjoy!

HOLLY GOLIGHTLY
Breakfast at Tiffany's (1961)

t is inconceivable to picture anyone but Hepburn as Manhattan party girl Holly Golightly, always on the hunt for a rich sugar daddy in Blake Edwards' classic adaptation of Truman Capote's novella, *Breakfast at Tiffany's* (1961). Although Capote thought she was all wrong for the part, moviegoers and critics disagreed, as did the Motion Picture Academy, which recognized Hepburn's irresistible performance with a Best Actress nomination — her fourth.

ELIZA DOOLITTLE
My Fair Lady (1964)

The casting of Hepburn in the plum role of Lerner and Loewe's *My Fair Lady* initially angered the musical's fans, who wanted Julie Andrews to reprise her star-making Broadway performance onscreen. Yet Hepburn rises to the daunting challenge of playing the Cockney flower girl who becomes a genteel society belle, under the strict tutelage of Professor Henry Higgins (Rex Harrison). Although her singing voice was dubbed by Marni Nixon, Hepburn excels in George Cukor's lavish, Academy Award-winning adaptation of

JOANNA WALLACE
Wait Until Dark (1967)

The same year Hepburn received her fifth Academy Award nomination for *Wait Until Dark* (1967), she gave what director Stanley Donen calls her best performance in *Two for the Road*. In the role of Joanna, Hepburn subtly reveals the conflicting emotions of a woman whose once-happy marriage has soured over time. This seriocomic and stylistically innovative portrait of a couple's rocky marriage pairs Hepburn with Albert Finney, who's equally brilliant as Joanna's arrogant but loving husband Mark.

PART 1

1948-1952

AUDREY HEPBURN:1948-1952

No one could have been more surprised at the success of her film career than Audrey Hepburn herself. To the young dancer and model, the words "film star" held no meaning. "Hollywood" — either as a place or as a concept — never entered her thoughts.

While the Hollywood Dream Factory was entering a nihilistic postwar period of *film noir* and romantic melodramas, half a world away, Hepburn and her mother, Ella, were just emerging from the very real darkness of World War II. Hepburn wanted nothing more than to become a ballerina. She and her mother moved to Amsterdam, where she studied under Sonia Gaskell. She later auditioned for Marie Rambert's ballet school in London and she was accepted on a scholarship. Ella could not afford to pay for Hepburn's travel or living expenses in London, though, and this may have proved fortuitous in launching Hepburn's film career.

HEPBURN'S EARLY FILM & STAGE ROLES

Laughter in Paradise (1951)

Hepburn has a walk-on role in this British comedy, starring Alastair Sim as a crime novelist who must act like one of his characters for a month to claim a £50,000 inheritance from an eccentric relative. Directed by Mario Zampi, *Laughter in Paradise* co-stars veteran character actors Joyce Grenfell and Ernest Thesiger in a breezy farce that did little to further Hepburn's screen career.

The Lavender Hill Mob (1951)

Portraying Chiquita, Hepburn briefly shares the screen with one of the giants of British cinema, Alec Guinness, in this comic gem from director Charles Crichton (*A Fish Called Wanda*). Guinness earned an Academy Award nomination for his virtuoso turn as a mild-mannered bank clerk plotting to steal gold bullion. *The Lavender Hill Mob* was the first Hepburn film distributed in the United States.

Young Wives' Tale (1951)

Scathingly dismissed by the *New York Times'* Bosley Crowther as "witless and foolish," this British comedy casts Hepburn as Eve, the sole unmarried resident of a boarding house. Playing a character Crowther describes as a "pretty young numbskull," Hepburn does what she can with a thankless supporting role in Henry Cass' film, which stars Joan Greenwood, best remembered for such films as *Kind Hearts and Coronets* (1949) and *Tom Jones* (1963).

A pair of Dutch filmmakers, director Charles Huguenot Van der Linden and Henry M. Josephson, was producing a low-budget travelogue of the Netherlands for Britain's Rank Film Studios. A flimsy plot, contrived to string together their fly-over shots of Dutch landscapes, required they hire "as many pretty girls as they could find." While there are several accounts about how Hepburn was actually discovered — some suggest that Van der Linden and Josephson actually visited Gaskell's studio — they all agree that Van der Linden was immediately taken with Hepburn, and that Hepburn took the job because she needed the money.

The resulting *Dutch in Seven Lessons* (1948), in which Hepburn played a coquettish flight attendant, proved to be a flop. Her appearance in it, however, led to various modeling jobs that helped pay her way to London and Marie Rambert's school. Although Hepburn often felt herself inferior to other dancers, she was cast in a series of musical productions, cabaret acts and revues, including shows for impresario Cecil Landeau. Audiences were captivated by her spirit — that *je ne sais quoi* quality — and of course, those wide, expressive eyes.

Monte Carlo Baby (1952)

Hepburn appears in both the English- and French-language versions of this wan comedy, co-directed by Jean Boyer and Lester Fuller. American actors Jules Munshin (*On the Town*) and Cara Williams try hard to pump up the laughs in the English-language version, but their efforts are mostly in vain. After Hepburn scored a smash in *Roman Holiday*, *Monte Carlo Baby* was released in the United States to cash in on her newfound fame.

Secret People (1952)

Of all the films Hepburn made before *Roman Holiday*, this suspense yarn holds up best. She portrays Nora Brentano, a ballet dancer whose older sister (Valentina Cortesa) gets embroiled with political assassins in London. Fourth-billed in the credits, Hepburn gives a solid performance that offers tantalizing hints of her dramatic potential. *Secret People* director Thorold Dickinson would subsequently play a pivotal role in Hepburn's securing the lead in *Roman Holiday*.

Gigi (1951)

The novice actress became the toast of Broadway for playing the title role in Anita Loos' adaptation of Colette's 1944 novella; MGM's musical version starring Leslie Caron would follow in 1958. As the 19th century Parisian courtesan-in-training, Hepburn won the 1952 Theatre World for *Gigi*, which debuted on Broadway on November 24, 1951, and ran for 219 performances.

Hepburn's "elf-like" countenance and innate sense of style soon graced the pages of British *Vogue*, and the British film industry took notice. Robert Lennard, casting director for Associated British Pictures Corporation (ABC), hired her for a bit part in *Laughter in Paradise* (1951), in which she played a cigarette girl whose fetching "Who wants a ciggy?" sales pitch was apparently enough to seal her destiny as an actress.

That same year, she appeared in Henry Cass' *Young Wives' Tale*. Though the film was released to dismal reviews, Hepburn, in a minor role as a typist, escaped critics' poisoned pens. ABC subsequently loaned her out to Ealing Studios, where Alec Guinness helped her get cast in *The Lavender Hill Mob* (1951), later named the British Film Academy's Best Film of 1951. And while there didn't seem to be anything special about Hepburn's bit role or her playing of it, there *was* something special about her.

Director Thorold Dickinson cast her in a meatier role as little sister to a political revolutionary in *Secret People* (1952). It mirrored Hepburn's own experiences as an aspiring dancer, and allowed her to showcase her ballet training, but the film's emotional climax unnerved her, stirring her own wartime memories. She doubted she could finish the scene. By the time cameras rolled, however, she summoned the professionalism and strength that would later define her — and played the scene as naturally and spontaneously as any seasoned veteran.

What followed, despite Hepburn's own misgivings, was a radical departure into fluff comedy. Shot in English- and French-language versions, *Monte Carlo Baby* (1952) was panned by the *New York Times* as a "seared desert of mediocrity," but Hepburn's 12-minute appearance as a movie star chasing after her missing baby would yield an opportunity she never would have imagined.

"What author ever expects to see one of his brain-children appear suddenly in the flesh? Not I, and yet, here it was. This unknown young woman was my own thoroughly French Gigi come alive!"

— Colette on Hepburn

Opposite page: A publicity still of Hepburn for *Secret People* (1952). Top: Cathleen Nesbit and Hepburn relax during a read-through of *Gigi*.

At that time, Broadway producers were adapting Sidonie-Gabrielle Colette's novel *Gigi* into a play. They had a problem, though — they had yet to find a suitable leading lady. In New York, 200 Equity actresses had been auditioned. Film star Leslie Caron had been dismissed as "*too* French." Serendipitously, the cast and crew of *Monte Carlo Baby* were migrating through the lobby of the hotel where Colette was vacationing. Colette's eyes fixed on the pixie dancing with a couple of musicians in the background. Gigi had come to miraculous life in the person of Audrey Hepburn. Hepburn's *Secret People* co-star Valentina Cortesa proclaimed it "Fortuna!"

Indeed, it would not be the last time "fortuna" smiled on Audrey Hepburn.

PART 2

1953-1959

AUDREY HEPBURN: 1953-1959

Of the fledgling celebrity, director Billy Wilder once quipped: "Don't wake my Sleeping Beauty. She doesn't know how big a star she really is." Indeed, with the release of *Roman Holiday* Audrey Hepburn seemed to have stepped into a fairy-existence — an international princess with a flourishing career, a startlingly level head her choice of princes. But for Hepburn and Hollywood, the 1950s would challenge and ape the fairy tale. It would be a decade of growing pains — a battle between tradition rebellion, duty and independence.

The Hollywood golden age was losing its luster. Hollywood had already endured the amount decrees" — court orders which forced a massive restructuring of the studio m and a divestiture from the studios' exhibition arms. Now it faced the twin threats of Carthyism and a small screen that proved to be a sleeping giant: television.

To lure audiences from their television sets, the studios tried several technologies and cs. Stereoscopic 3-D was one of the first. A short-lived craze, however, it eventually to its rival: CinemaScope.

HEPBURN'S LEADING MEN, 1953-1959

ASTAIRE
Face (1957)

cusp of 60 when he partnered epburn in *Funny Face*, Astaire with ageless grace in this delight-ical, loosely based on the 1927 ay hit. The very same year he epburn off her feet, Astaire would th Cyd Charisse in *Silk Stockings*, al version of Greta Garbo's 1939

HUMPHREY BOGART
Sabrina (1954)

After he played the psychotic Captain Queeg in *The Caine Mutiny* (1954), Bogart revealed his softer side oppo-site Hepburn in *Sabrina*. Although they famously didn't click offscreen, Bogart and Hepburn make an inspired, if offbeat romantic team in Billy Wilder's classic film, later remade with Harrison Ford and

GARY COOPER
Love in the Afternoon (1957)

Trading his saddle and spurs for elegantly tailored suits, Gary Cooper took a break from making westerns to woo Hepburn in Billy Wilder's sophisticated Parisian romance. Then in his midfifties but still dashingly handsome, the two-time Academy Award winner would return to the Western genre for his follow-up film,

Introduced to audiences in the biblical epic *The Robe* (1953), CinemaScope morphed film's standard aspect ratio from 4:3 to a widescreen 2.55:1 (later adjusted down to 2.35:1), allowing filmmakers to paint sweeping panoramas. The format proved to be a hit, and by 1957, nearly every studio employed it in blockbuster historical epics, westerns and musicals.

At the same time, filmmakers were finding greater artistic license in the kinds of stories they told. The success of several foreign films — unblessed by the Production Code's Seal of Approval — led to direct challenges to the Code itself. Otto Preminger openly rebelled by producing two films that would go unapproved and on to commercial success: *The Moon Is Blue* (1953) and *The Man with the Golden Arm* (1955). Other filmmakers followed suit, and the Code soon lost its authoritarian hold on Hollywood. By the late 1950s, the deaths of Hollywood moguls Louis B. Mayer and Columbia president Harry Cohn seemed to herald the true end of Hollywood's golden age, opening the doors to the rebel filmmakers of the 1960s and '70s.

In 1953, however, Hepburn was just embarking on this whirlwind journey. Nominated for her role in *Roman Holiday,* and committed to a road tour of *Gigi,*

HENRY FONDA
War and Peace (1956)

Riding high on the success of *Mister Roberts* (1955), Fonda joined Hepburn and Mel Ferrer in Italy to shoot King Vidor's ambitious adaptation of Tolstoy's epic novel. Playing a role reportedly intended for Peter Ustinov, Fonda nevertheless brings conviction to his scenes with a radiant Hepburn, cast as the aris-

WILLIAM HOLDEN
Sabrina (1954)

Teaming with director Billy Wilder for the third time on *Sabrina,* the Academy Award–winning star of *Stalag 17* (1953) fell hopelessly in love with Hepburn during production — much to the chagrin of co-star Bogart. Then one of Hollywood's most popular stars, Holden would score three other hits in 1954: *The Bridges at*

GREGORY PECK
Roman Holiday (1953)

The handsome embodiment of sincerity onscreen, Peck graciously cedes the spotlight to Hepburn in William Wyler's beloved romantic comedy, shot on location in the fabled "City of Seven Hills." Nominated five times for an Academy Award, Peck would finally win the Best Actor statuette for *To Kill a Mockingbird*

Hepburn saw her relationship with British lord James Hanson crack under the pressure of her relentless work schedule. The two parted amicably, but it wouldn't be long before she caught the eye of not one, but two, leading men. *Sabrina* co-star (and notorious playboy) William Holden regarded Hepburn as the "love of his life." That he was already married to actress Brenda Marshall didn't seem to weigh upon his conscience. For Hepburn, however, sex was "overrated," and she enjoyed a largely platonic affair with Holden for the duration of *Sabrina*'s production.

Her true "Prince Charming" would come in the person of actor-director Mel Ferrer, whom she met in London at a release party for *Roman Holiday*. Like Hepburn, he came from upper-class stock, and had a background in theater (most notably as a founder of the La Jolla Playhouse). He enjoyed early success as an actor in films such as *Lost Boundaries* (1949) and *The Brave Bulls* (1951), but his magical turn in *Lili* (1953) thoroughly enthralled the "incorrigibly" romantic Hepburn. The chemistry between them was immediate, and they married September 24, 1954.

They aspired to be the next Olivier and Leigh, and Ferrer often sought projects in which they both could star. They appeared on Broadway together in the French play *Ondine* in 1954 and went on to star together in *War and Peace* (1956) and the television

"I know I'm not very well built. I'm not very shapely and not very voluptuous…. It may be that the accent has gone off sex slightly and gone on to femininity."

— Hepburn, on how she impacted fashion and beauty in the 1950s

Opposite page: Astaire and Hepburn in *Funny Face* (1957). Top: Ready for her close-up: Hepburn on the set of *Roman Holiday* (1953).

production of *Mayerling* (1957). It was clear from the start, however, that Hepburn's star shone brighter than his, and he retreated behind the camera, choosing to direct her in 1959's *Green Mansions*.

For as many film roles as Hepburn accepted, she turned down nearly as many. Citing an unwillingness to relive her war experiences, she turned down the lead role in *The Diary of Anne Frank* (1959) and a non-musical biography of Maria von Trapp. Critics questioned whether she turned down roles because they meant a long separation from Ferrer, or if the domineering Ferrer were calling the shots — rejecting projects that didn't include roles for him. Hepburn was quick to scoff at such conjecture, and attempted to quash the rumors in every interview.

But as independent as she seemed in her career, in her personal life, she was a traditional and dutiful spouse, attentive to her husband's needs and often placing them above her own. And more than anything, she wanted to be a mother. She miscarried in 1954, but in 1959, fortune smiled upon her. She turned down historic roles in *Cleopatra* (1963) and Robert Wise's *West Side Story* (1961). She was pregnant again, and work was not going to jeopardize her child's health. The wisp of a girl with whom the world fell in love in the early 1950s was, by decade's end, finally growing up.

ROMAN HOLIDAY (1953)

PARAMOUNT PICTURES

DIRECTOR: WILLIAM WYLER

SCREENPLAY: IAN MCLELLAN HUNTER AND JOHN DIGHTON

STORY: DALTON TRUMBO (CREDITED TO IAN MCLELLAN HUNTER)

PRINCIPAL CAST: AUDREY HEPBURN (PRINCESS ANN/ANYA SMITH), GREGORY PECK (JOE BRADLEY) AND EDDIE ALBERT (IRVING RADOVICH)

After a handful of bit parts and supporting roles in British films, Audrey Hepburn catapulted from obscurity to international stardom as the runaway princess in *Roman Holiday*. While it's now unthinkable to imagine anyone else playing Princess Ann, Hepburn took a circuitous path to making her major motion picture debut in this classic romantic comedy, which the American Film Institute named the fourth greatest love story of all time in 2002.

When two-time Academy Award–winning director William Wyler began searching for just the right actress to play *Roman Holiday's* heroine, he initially considered both Jean Simmons and Elizabeth Taylor for the role. When neither actress was available, he turned to Hepburn, an unknown then preparing to make her Broadway stage debut in *Gigi*. Since Wyler was unable to conduct Hepburn's screen test in London, however, he asked British filmmaker Thorold Dickinson — who had directed Hepburn in *Secret People* (1952) — to film the screen novice's audition.

Top: Princess Ann (Hepburn) makes her entrance at a state occasion. Bottom: A petulant princess at the end of the day.

Arriving at Pinewood Studios with her lines fully memorized, Hepburn gave a competent if uninspired audition that offered little indication of the spark Dickinson knew she could bring to the role. He therefore kept the camera rolling after the test concluded; unaware that she was being filmed, Hepburn relaxed and came across as utterly beguiling and vibrantly alive — the very qualities Wyler was looking for in his heroine.

The rare studio film of its era shot on location, *Roman Holiday* begins with Princess Ann (Hepburn) formally greeting what seems like an endless line of dignitaries at her country's grandiose Roman embassy. Although exhausted from a lengthy goodwill tour, she dutifully follows protocol. However, back in her own room, she breaks down in a tearful rage against the grinding schedule she must follow. Alarmed, her doctor gives her a sedative and leaves her alone to sleep, but the princess is not tired. She sneaks out of the embassy and makes her way through the lively Roman streets. Eventually, the sedative takes effect and she stretches out for a nap on a stone wall.

Luckily for her, American reporter Joe Bradley (Gregory Peck) walks by. At first he is understandably reluctant to become involved with this well-dressed, poetry-quoting and clearly intoxicated girl, but he soon decides to take her home, where she passes out on his couch. The next morning, Joe reports late to work, only to have his editor throw a newspaper reporting that Princess Ann has taken ill and canceled all her

Top: American journalist Joe Bradley (Gregory Peck) befriends the tipsy princess. Bottom: Joe finds himself with an unexpected house guest.

Joe gets an earful from his editor (Hartley Power) about the runaway princess.

engagements. One look at the front-page picture and Joe realizes that the girl sleeping off a bender is none other than her royal highness.

Immediately, he calls his photographer buddy Irving Radovich (Albert) and tells him he has a big story that Irving must capture on film. With Irving tagging along, Joe later meets Princess Ann on the Spanish Steps, where they begin a day-long exploration of Rome. Freed from responsibility, Princess Ann dives into the adventure. Whether it's savoring a gelato, sipping champagne, or racing off on a Vespa, she approaches every new experience with such enthusiasm that it leaves Joe breathless. A romance blooms, but at day's end, both Princess Ann and Joe face difficult choices: she must choose between love and duty, while Joe must decide whether to run the blockbuster story that could make his career, but ruin the princess.

Although many established stars might have scoffed at the prospect of sharing the screen with a novice, Peck quickly became one of Hepburn's most ardent fans early in the production. In fact, he called his agent and insisted that Hepburn be

"I'd like to do just whatever I like the whole day long!"

— Princess Ann (Hepburn)

given equal, above-the-title billing, because "this girl is going to win the Academy Award in her first role." It was a rare act of chivalry in an industry where backstabbing and upstaging co-stars were par for the course.

When *Roman Holiday* premiered on August 27, 1953, critics and moviegoers embraced the unusual, Belgian-born beauty as readily as Peck. As noted film critic Molly Haskell reflected, "She set her own pace and style with a look that decidedly ran counter to then-prevailing standards of female beauty. She was patrician, exotic, [and] boyishly slender at a time when the accent was on big-breasted bombshells and girl-next-door types." A.H. Weiler, a film critic for the *New York Times,* wrote in his 1953 review that Hepburn was a "slender, elfin and wistful beauty." Although savvy enough to recognize a flaw or two in the film, Weiler clearly fell under *Roman Holiday*'s spell: "It is a contrived fable but a bittersweet legend with laughs that leaves the spirits soaring."

At the time *Roman Holiday* was released, a bittersweet love story mirroring Hepburn and Peck's screen romance was unfolding on the world stage. In England, Princess Margaret began a romance with Peter Townsend, a divorced commoner who held a prestigious position with the royal family. Although thousands followed the courtship and believed it would end in marriage, Princess Margaret ultimately ended their engagement in 1955, citing the need to place duty over love.

Nominated for ten Academy Awards, including Best Picture, *Roman Holiday* won three of the coveted statuettes. As Gregory Peck had

Top: The princess contemplates her new hairdo. Bottom: Hepburn and Peck on Rome's legendary Spanish Steps.

predicted, Hepburn won the Best Actress award; she had previously won both the Golden Globe and the New York Film Critics Best Actress prize. The legendary Edith Head won the fifth of her eight Oscars for Best Costume Design. And in a category whose real nominee was not revealed for several decades, the award for Best Writing, Motion Picture Story went to Ian McLellan Hunter. In reality, Dalton Trumbo wrote the *Roman Holiday* screenplay. Then facing a year in jail for refusing to testify before the House Committee for Un-American Activities, Trumbo asked Hunter to "front" for him. As a blacklisted, suspected Communist, Dalton Trumbo did not receive proper recognition from the Academy until 1992.

"This girl is going to win the Academy Award in her first role."

— Gregory Peck on Hepburn

Opposite page: The princess
and Joe embark on a day of
adventure. Top: Joe convinces
his photographer friend Irving
Radovich (Eddie Albert) to help
him with his story on Princess
Ann. Bottom: A wild ride
through the streets of Rome.

Roman Holiday was a commercial and critical hit in its day and has remained a beloved classic. Viewed today, the relationship between Audrey Hepburn and Gregory Peck is as compelling as it was for audiences in the 1950s. Their chemistry builds from a sweet and bemused beginning to a convincing and palpable longing. Stepping into a role that Cary Grant turned down, Peck delivers an understated and reserved performance that balances and offsets Hepburn's dazzling charm. It was a wise decision on his part, as it is hard to compete with the emotional delicacy and mischievous spirit that Audrey Hepburn brings to Princess Ann.

Roman Holiday marked the beginning of a collaboration between Audrey Hepburn and director William Wyler that would yield two more films, *The Children's Hour* (1961) and *How to Steal a Million* (1966).

Princess Ann and Joe share a tender moment dancing under the stars.

Top: Princess Ann with her royal handlers. Bottom: Peck at the bittersweet conclusion of *Roman Holiday*.

"It's too much. I want to say thank you to everybody, who these past months and years have helped, guided and given me so much. I am truly, truly grateful and terribly happy."

— Hepburn, accepting the Best Actress Academy Award for *Roman Holiday*

SABRINA (1954)

PARAMOUNT PICTURES
DIRECTOR: BILLY WILDER
SCREENPLAY: BILLY WILDER, SAMUEL TAYLOR AND ERNEST LEHMAN
BASED ON THE PLAY "SABRINA FAIR" BY TAYLOR
PRINCIPAL CAST: HUMPHREY BOGART (LINUS LARRABEE), AUDREY HEPBURN (SABRINA FAIRCHILD), WILLIAM HOLDEN (DAVID LARRABEE), WALTER HAMPDEN (MR. LARRABEE), JOHN WILLIAMS (THOMAS FAIRCHILD), MARTHA HYER (ELIZABETH TYSON), NELLA WALKER (MRS. LARRABEE) AND FRANCIS X. BUSHMAN (MR. TYSON)

Roman Holiday (1953) may have been the proverbial hard act to follow, but *Sabrina* earned Audrey Hepburn another Best Actress Academy Award nomination and provided a similar showcase for her singular charms. In Billy Wilder's frothy romantic comedy, the star projects the same irresistible combination of girl/woman, commoner/sophisticate, and innocent/desirable that audiences loved in *Roman Holiday*. Paramount was so certain that *Sabrina* was the perfect follow-up for Hepburn that the studio bought the rights to Samuel Taylor's play, *Sabrina Fair*, even before it premiered on Broadway.

Through no fault of her own, Hepburn was quickly becoming the poster child for May-December screen romances. After sharing the screen with Gregory Peck, 13 years her senior, the 24-year-old Hepburn found herself teamed with 54-year-old Humphrey Bogart in *Sabrina*. Alongside the craggy-faced Bogart, she seems even more

Top: Even barefoot and washing cars, Hepburn as the waiflike Sabrina exudes a captivating charm. Bottom: The *uber*-rich Larrabee family poses for a portrait: Linus (Humphrey Bogart), parents Oliver (Walter Hampden) and Maude (Nella Walker), and David (William Holden).

breathlessly wide-eyed and in love with life. So if, as a reviewer for the *Chicago Daily Tribune* observed, there are times in *Sabrina* when "the camera lingers lovingly and sometimes overlong" on Hepburn and her dreamy countenance, Wilder and cinematographer Charles Lang can be forgiven.

It wasn't just an adoring public that was smitten by her; Hepburn cast an equally potent spell over her directors, cinematographers and co-stars too. In fact, she became romantically involved with co-star William Holden very early into the production of *Sabrina*, a film that cemented her status as one of Hollywood's glitterati.

In a pre–Academy Award *New York Times* story, Bosley Crowther gushed that *Sabrina* was "one of the juiciest of its nectarine kind in years," adding that "Audrey Hepburn's limpid performance as a chic Cinderella on a classy Long Island estate is up to her very memorable acting of the princess in *Roman Holiday*." This time, however, she portrays a commoner who would be a princess, rather than the other way around. Still, the film begins with a Hepburn-as-Sabrina voiceover narration ("Once upon a time, on the north shore of Long Island . . .") that lets viewers know it's only a matter of cinematic time before this chauffeur's daughter assumes her rightful place as a modern-day princess.

Our first glimpse of Sabrina is a memorable one. Barefoot, she's helping her father (John Williams) wash his employer's eight cars while the Larrabee family

Top: Sabrina spies on the Larrabees' party, wondering what it would be like to be one of the "beautiful people." Bottom: David Larrabee and his latest conquest at his favorite indoor tennis court rendezvous.

hosts a lavish party on the grounds of their Long Island estate (the actual home of Paramount chairman Barney Balaban). In a flash Sabrina is in a tree where she can get a better look at the blue-blood socialites flirting with the object of her unrequited affection: David Larrabee (Holden). It's a simple scene, yet ir conveys a wealth of information about Sabrina: her rags-to-riches longing; the tomboy past she's enjoyed on the grounds with both David and his older brother Linus (Bogart); the torch she carries for David; the close relationship she has with her father; and a hint of the metamorphosis that's soon to occur.

The plot turns on a romantic comedy cliché: the eternal triangle. The Larrabees have their hands in all sorts of enterprises and own a skyscraper headquarters, but their oldest son Linus is the only one who actually works. Young David is a playboy whose standard ploy is to cut an attractive socialite from the blossoming herd and have her meet him at the family's indoor tennis court for champagne and a slow dance to prearranged orchestra music ("Isn't It Romantic") — a literal *courting* ritual. Here, too, Sabrina is a wide-eyed spectator, peering through the window and wishing it were her, never perceiving David's insincerity.

Sabrina tries to end her unrequited love for David. Wilder wrote as he shot and at one point asked Hepburn to fake an illness to buy him more time.

"He's still David Larrabee and you're still the chauffeur's daughter, and you're still reaching for the moon."

— Fairchild (John Williams)

But fairy tales are meant to engage the audience, and as viewers watch poor Sabrina pine for David, leave for Paris, and return a glamorous woman, they're perfectly happy to have Linus insist that David marry socialite Elizabeth Tyson (Martha Hyer) to cement a merger, then woo Sabrina himself after David finally falls for her, ostensibly to keep her from getting in the way of the family business. While Linus is set up as the nice guy no one wants to see finish last, as a number of reviewers pointed out, the ensuing Sabrina-Linus romance would have been more believable had Cary Grant not pulled out of the project only a week before filming began.

Shot in Long Island over seven weeks during fall 1953 on a $2 million budget (larger than *Roman Holiday*), *Sabrina* received Academy Award nominations for Best Actress, Director, Screenplay, Art Direction, Cinematography and Costume Design. Only Edith Head won, for Best Costume Design — an ironic victory, considering that Hepburn requested and received permission to shop in Paris for her own wardrobe. The young star commissioned Hubert de Givenchy (who went uncredited) to design the clothes her character wears when she returns from cooking school in Paris a dramatically changed woman.

Black-and-white is the perfect showcase for detective stories and beautiful women, and Hepburn looks striking in so many frames, whether dressed in plain peasant garb or the latest French styles. Wilder pulls in for numerous tight close-ups, so the audience has the sensation of being slowly drawn in by her bright mesmerizing eyes and easy smile. The challenge for Wilder and Head was to costume and film Hepburn so that she looked waiflike rather than bone-thin, and

Top: Sent to Paris to become a cook like her mother, Sabrina instead begins her journey toward sophistication. Bottom: Ugly duckling no more: Sabrina dazzles at the Larrabees' high-society party.

barefoot without highlighting her big feet. But that problem paled compared to behind-the-scenes politics.

According to *Sabrina* co-star Martha Hyer, "there was much friction, side-taking, and intrigue during the filming," with Bogart "almost paranoid" that his two co-stars and director were against him. The three drank martinis together after the wrap, leaving Bogie to imbibe with other crew and cast. Already feeling uncomfortable about the age difference with Hepburn that probably caused Grant to bolt at the last minute, Bogie became even more annoyed when his co-stars began their affair. Hyer said that when Hepburn uncharacteristically flubbed a line,

"No, Father, the moon is reaching for me."

— Sabrina (Hepburn)

Opposite page: Linus and Sabrina sailing on Long Island sound. Top: "They'll say I'm too young for you. There'll be an awful scandal." Wilder relied heavily on shadows and conceals for this crucial scene. Bottom: Although married, Holden fell deeply in love with Hepburn during the filming of *Sabrina*.

Bogart deadpanned, "Maybe you should stay home and study your lines instead of going out every night."

Despite the tension, when cameras rolled the stars shined, and *Sabrina* remains one of Hepburn's most delightful romantic comedies. The second Best Actress nomination secured her status as a major star, but more importantly, *Sabrina* also solidified Hepburn's image as the most strikingly beautiful "nice girl" in Hollywood.

"Have I changed? Have I really changed?"

— Sabrina (Hepburn)

Opposite page: Linus and
Sabrina fall in love. Off-camera,
there was no love lost between
Bogart and Hepburn. Top:
An infatuated David drives
Sabrina home from the train
station. Bottom: Sabrina writes
her father and the rest of the
Larrabee servants from Paris.

"Audrey knew that the
true arc of her character
hinged upon her
dazzling transformation
from waifish to
wonderful."

— Uncredited narrator, *Sabrina
Documentary*, Paramount Home
Video

WAR AND PEACE (1956)

PARAMOUNT PICTURES

DIRECTOR: KING VIDOR

SCREENPLAY: BRIDGET BOLAND, ROBERT WESTERBY, KING VIDOR, MARIO CAMERINI, ENNIO DE CONCINI AND IVO PERILLI

BASED ON THE NOVEL BY LEO TOLSTOY

PRINCIPAL CAST: AUDREY HEPBURN (NATASHA ROSTOVA), HENRY FONDA (PIERRE BEZUKHOV), MEL FERRER (PRINCE ANDREY BOLKONSKY) VITTORIO GASSMAN (ANATOLE KURAGIN), HERBERT LOM (NAPOLEON BONAPARTE), OSCAR HOMOLKA (GEN MIKHAIL KUTUZOV), ANITA EKBERG (HELENE KURAGINA), JEREMY BRETT (NICHOLAS ROSTOV) AND JOHN MILLS (PLATON)

After playing a princess and a Long Island Cinderella in *Roman Holiday* (1953) and *Sabrina* (1954) respectively, Audrey Hepburn was Hollywood's "It" girl — an elegant sylph whose Old World manners and graceful bearing set her apart from such contemporaries as Marilyn Monroe, Debbie Reynolds and Elizabeth Taylor. Rather than coast on her effervescent charm in romantic comedies, however, Hepburn chose to tackle the first important dramatic role of her career in King Vidor's opulent Technicolor adaptation of Leo Tolstoy's epic masterpiece, *War and Peace*.

A perennial fixture on literary critics' list of the world's great novels, Tolstoy's sprawling yet intimate narrative about the interwoven lives of three aristocratic Russian families during the Napoleonic era had long been the dream project of such filmmakers as Elia Kazan, Orson Welles and Fred Zinnemann. Producers David O. Selznick and Mike Todd also saw *War and Peace* as prime material for a sweeping, wide-screen epic that would lure

Top: Natasha Rostova (Hepburn) rejoices over the returning Russian troops. Bottom: Natasha pines over Prince Andrey (Mel Ferrer).

fifties-era audiences away from their televisions. But it was two, then little-known Italian producers, Dino De Laurentiis and Carlo Ponti, who finally convinced Paramount Pictures that they could transform Tolstoy's nearly 600,000-word novel into a commercial film with a running time of less than four hours. They hired a team of writers, including novelist Irwin Shaw (who later demanded that his name be taken off the credits) to streamline *War and Peace* for veteran director King Vidor, whose erratic track record ran the gamut from classics (1928's *The Crowd*) to kitsch (1946's *Duel in the Sun*).

Six screenwriters eventually received credit for adapting *War and Peace*, which stars Hepburn as the vivacious aristocrat Natasha Rostova, betrothed in marriage to the soldier Prince Andrey (Mel Ferrer). In a role originally intended for Peter Ustinov, Henry Fonda plays the hedonistic intellectual Pierre Bezukhov, whose unrequited love for Natasha drives him into an unhappy marriage with the beautiful but treacherous Helene (Swedish sexpot Anita Ekberg, who replaced Arlene Dahl). Meanwhile, Helene's brother, the libertine Anatole (Vittorio Gassman), seduces Natasha, thereby jeopardizing her marriage to Prince Andrey. Against the backdrop of the Napoleonic Wars — re-created in spectacular battle scenes featuring the Italian Army as Russian and French soldiers — these Russian aristocrats struggle to hold onto their way of life, despite the looming threat of Napoleon (Herbert Lom).

Top: Natasha attends her first ball with Nicholas Rostov (Jeremy Brett) and Sonya Rostova (May Britt). Bottom: *War and Peace* marked the first and only time Hepburn and husband Mel Ferrer acted together on the big screen. They later reteamed for a television production of *Mayerling*.

Shot in Italy by gifted cinematographer Jack Cardiff, *War and Peace* was a physically and emotionally demanding production that took a toll on everyone, especially Hepburn, who had suffered a miscarriage earlier that year. Wearing heavy winter costumes made of fur and velvet during the intense heat of summer exhausted the star, who barely escaped serious injury when a horse fainted, nearly rolling over her during the filming of a hunting scene. The battle scenes also dredged up painful childhood memories of World War II and gave her nightmares. Exacerbating these physical and emotional challenges was the fact that most of Hepburn's scenes were shot out of sequence — a departure from the chronological shooting schedule of her previous two films.

That said, there was a sizable reward for enduring the rigors and frustrations of the six-month shoot of *War and Peace*: a jaw-dropping salary of $350,000, the highest fee paid to any actress in the world up to that time. Hepburn exercised her star clout by insisting that the producers hire Alberto and Grazia de Rossi to oversee her hair and makeup (she would work with the couple

"When I finally say I love you to any man and really mean it, it will be like a defeated general who's lost all his troops, surrendering and handing his sword to the enemy."

— Natasha (Hepburn)

for the rest of her career). She also asked friend and designer Hubert de Givenchy to supervise her 24 costume fittings on *War and Peace*.

According to the *Saturday Review*, Vidor's rough cut ran approximately five and a half hours. When it finally opened in August of 1956, the $6 million-budgeted *War and Peace* clocked in at 208 minutes. Although *Variety*'s critic pronounced it "three-and-a-half hours of vivid cinematic magic," other critics balked at the liberties taken with Tolstoy's narrative, the excessive running time and the cast's mishmash of accents, most notably John Mills' cockney burr. These criticisms were not shared by Tolstoy's daughter Alexandra, who declared that Vidor's *War and Peace* "caught the spirit of my father which permeates the pages of the novel."

Her endorsement notwithstanding, Vidor's *War and Peace* is marred by a dramatically stilted first act and consistently poor looping; the dialogue in some of the outdoor scenes sounds like it was re-recorded in a studio echo chamber. Fonda is also too old and physically imposing for the role of Pierre, who's an overweight and socially awkward intellectual in the pages of Tolstoy's novel. To his credit, Fonda tries hard to suggest Pierre's naiveté and wears padding to appear overweight, but he never comes across as anything but miscast.

If Fonda is out of his dramatic element in *War and Peace*, Hepburn is simply exquisite as Natasha. While it might be argued that she lacked the maturity to convey the character's full emotional arc from entitled innocent to a

Opposite page: The Italian Army plays both the Russian and French forces in *War and Peace.* Top: Natasha lends a helping hand to a band of soldiers returning from the front. Bottom: Natasha watches over an ailing Prince Andrey.

woman scarred by war and lost love — Hepburn was 25 years old at the time — she effortlessly holds the screen with her vivid, heartfelt performance in *War and Peace*.

Despite its many flaws, *War and Peace* is still an impressive example of filmmaking on a grand scale. Vidor received his fifth and final Academy Award nomination for Best Director (he lost to George Stevens for *Giant*). The Motion Picture Academy also recognized Jack Cardiff and costume designer Marie De Matteis with nominations for Best Cinematography and Best Costume Design, respectively.

"I'm not worth it — it's impossible! Please don't tell anyone!"

— Hepburn on learning she was to be paid a salary of $350,000 for her role in *War and Peace*

"She dominates an epic picture by refusing to distort her character to the epic mould, letting her…very littleness in the face of history captivate us by its humanity contrasted with the inhumanity of war."

— *Films in Review*, on Hepburn's rendering of Natasha

Opposite page: In the aftermath of war, Natasha returns home to unsettling circumstances. Top: Four years before she played herself in Fellini's *La Dolce Vita* (1960), Anita Ekberg portrayed Helene Kuragina in *War and Peace*. Bottom: Mel Ferrer as Prince Andrey.

Top: A spectacular ballroom scene from *War and Peace*, one of the most expensive films of the 1950s. Bottom: British actor Herbert Lom as Napoleon. Opposite: Natasha with her dear friend Pierre (Henry Fonda).

"Did you notice he almost never smiles? While I was singing, I turned around suddenly and caught him looking at me and he was smiling then. And I felt — but it's almost impossible to describe — I felt as if someone had given me the most enormous, beautiful present."

— Natasha Rostova (Hepburn)

Today, most critics and film historians point to Sergei Bondarchuk's monumental, Academy Award winning Soviet film version of *War and Peace* (1968) as the definitive screen treatment of Tolstoy's novel. Yet Hepburn's performance in Vidor's 1956 film still lights up the screen, more than a half century after she received Best Actress nominations from the New York Film Critics, the Hollywood Foreign Press Association and the British Academy of Film and Television Awards for *War and Peace*. As the reviewer for the British *Films in Review* so accurately and succinctly put it, "She incarnates all that is worth fighting for."

"The Greatest Novel Ever Written ... Now Magnificently Alive On The Screen!"

— *War and Peace* tagline

Funny Face (1957)

Paramount Pictures

Director: Stanley Donen

Screenplay: Leonard Gershe

Principal Cast: Audrey Hepburn (Jo Stockton), Fred Astaire (Dick Avery), Kay Thompson (Maggie Prescott), Michel Auclair (Professor Emil Flostre) and Robert Flemyng (Paul Duval)

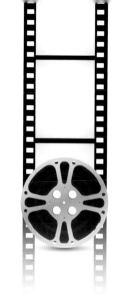

There is a certain delicious irony to Audrey Hepburn's star turn in Stanley Donen's irresistible 1957 musical *Funny Face*. The actress who declared that wearing couture made her feel safe plays a girl who could not give a fig about designer duds, even as she becomes a *Vogue*-like fashion magazine's new icon. As the waif who conquers Paris and captures Fred Astaire's heart, the charming gamine lights up the screen in one of the last of the great musicals of Hollywood's golden age.

In a way, the witty, romantic *Funny Face* is a spin on the ugly duckling story, except in this case, Greenwich Village bookseller Jo Stockton (Hepburn) is already a swan. At least that's how fashion photographer Dick Avery (Astaire) sees her, when he and imperious, Diana Vreeland-like magazine editor Maggie Prescott (saloon singer and *Eloise* creator Kay Thompson) first meet the beatnik beauty during a photo shoot.

Top: *Quality* magazine editor Maggie Prescott (Kay Thompson) urges her staff and America's women to "Think Pink." Bottom: Photographer Dick Avery (Fred Astaire) and Maggie Prescott invade the "sinister" Greenwich Village bookshop where Jo Stockton (Hepburn) works.

However, Dick is very much in the minority about Jo's prospects as a cover girl for Maggie's fashion magazine, *Quality*. "I think her face is perfectly funny," Maggie says, a sentiment shared by Jo herself. Jo finds the fashion world altogether silly, anyway. But when she discovers this modeling assignment will take her to the City of Light, home of her idol, Professor Emile Flostre (Michel Auclair), a philosopher who preaches something called "empathicalism," she is willing to compromise her lofty ideals to walk the runway. Of course, it doesn't hurt that she gets to spend time with Dick, who caught her eye from the moment he, Maggie and a gaggle of models invaded her Greenwich Village bookshop.

Funny Face borrowed a star — Astaire — and some of the George and Ira Gershwin songs from a 1927 Broadway musical of the same name, while songwriter Roger Edens and screenwriter Leonard Gershe contributed a handful of new tunes. In a way, the movie is a happy accident. It very nearly did not get made at all when MGM passed on the original leading lady, *The Pajama Game* star Carol Haney. It was Gershe who suggested Hepburn, but getting her meant that *Funny Face* would not be an MGM musical at all. She was under contract to Paramount and the studio was not interested in loaning her out. Instead, MGM had to be magnanimous and lend out Donen, Gershe, and Edens in order for the film to go forward.

Thirty-three-year-old, trend-setting fashion photographer Richard Avedon was Gershe's template for the

Top: "I felt that you wanted to be kissed," Dick tells a surprised Jo. Bottom: When it comes to Jo's makeover, Maggie is hands-on.

dashing shutterbug Avery, a stark contrast to the debonair, but 57-year-old Astaire. Donen wanted Hepburn and Hepburn wanted Astaire, confiding to her husband, actor Mel Ferrer, "This is it! I don't sing well enough, but oh if only I can do this with Fred Astaire."

Hepburn may not have thought much of herself as a singer, but she had trained as a dancer until injury forced her to change careers. Astaire was a longtime idol. In 1981, 25 years after they made *Funny Face,* she presented him with the American Film Institute's Lifetime Achievement Award, and recalled her nerves the first time they danced together on a Paramount rehearsal stage. "I could feel myself turn into solid lead, while my heart sank into my own two left feet. Then suddenly I felt a hand around my waist and with his inimitable grace and lightness, Fred literally swept me off my feet. I experienced the thrill that all women at some point in their lives have dreamed of — to dance just once with Fred Astaire."

Shooting the movie itself was not so glamorous, particularly when it came time to film Hepburn and Astaire's big romantic number, the Gershwins' "He Loves and

Maggie, Dick, and Jo find they have something in common — utter joy at being in Paris.

"Audrey was the first actress to play a fashion model on-screen who really could have been one offscreen."

—— *Funny Face* screenwriter Leonard Gershe

She Loves," in a Paris meadow. Hepburn wears a wedding dress in the scene, part of her modeling assignment, the outfit bringing out Jo and Dick's feelings. An unseasonably rainy spring refused to cooperate. It rained for four weeks straight. When Donen was finally able to shoot the scene in which the couple sing and dance across a verdant field, it was all they could do to keep their balance among the ooze.

"Here I have waited 20 years to dance with Fred Astaire, and what do I get? Mud!" sighed Hepburn.

Whatever difficulties Donen and his cast faced in making the movie, none of it is evident on the screen in a lighter-than-air confection that takes the action from uptown Manhattan to bohemian Greenwich Village and from the top of the Eiffel Tower and a fashion designer's atelier to a real gone Left Bank dive and a philosopher's salon. The film's March 1957 opening left the *New York Times'* Bosley Crowther enchanted, declaring, "It is reasonable to reckon that you won't see a prettier musical film — or one more extraordinarily stylish — during the balance of this year." *Variety* was less enthusiastic, but still allowed, "This is a lightly diverting, modish, Parisian-localed tintuner." More recently, *Time Out's* Stephen Garrett raved, "The musical that dares to rhyme Sartre with Montmartre, *Funny Face* — surprisingly from Paramount rather than MGM —- knocks most other musicals off the screen for its visual beauty, its witty panache, and its totally uncalculating charm."

Gershe received an Academy Award nomination for his screenplay, and there were nominations for Ray June's cinematography,

Top: In a smoky Paris bistro, Jo teaches Dick a thing or two about self-expression. Bottom: Dick woos Jo with a buoyant dance.

"Every girl on every page of *Quality* has grace, elegance and pizzazz. Now what's wrong with bringing out a girl who has character, spirit and intelligence?"

—— Photographer Dick Avery (Fred Astaire) on Jo Stockton (Hepburn)

Top: The beatnik Jo transformed into "a bird of paradise," according to wowed designer Paul Duval (Robert Flemyng). Bottom: Hepburn upstages the third-century BC marble statue *Winged Victory of Samothrace* in one of the film's most iconic images. Opposite page: A jealous Dick discovers Jo in conference with her philosopher idol Prof. Emile Flostre (Michel Auclair).

Givenchy and Edith Head's costumes, and for art direction, but none for its stars. Nevertheless, *Funny Face* was a triumph for Hepburn that gave her ample opportunity to prove that she could in fact sing and dance. Granted, her singing voice is thin, but she brings real feeling to the Gershwin standard "How Long Has This Been Going On?" and performs a charming duet of "S'Wonderful" with Astaire. That said, Hepburn's musical talents evidently failed to impress director George Cukor, who would later hire Marni Nixon to dub Hepburn's songs for *My Fair Lady* (1964).

"Audrey was always more about fashion than movies or acting."

— *Funny Face* director Stanley Donen

Funny Face was one of two films Hepburn shot in Paris that year (the other being Billy Wilder's *Love in the Afternoon*). The City of Light seemed like the perfect backdrop for the incandescent star, who would return to Paris to make both *Charade* (1963) and *How to Steal a Million* (1966). As she sings in *Funny Face*, "When they parlez-vous me, then I gotta confess. That's for me: Bonjour, Paris!" Hepburn, no doubt, would second that sentiment.

Hepburn relied on her ballet training to partner with Astaire for this number, shot in a rain-soaked meadow.

Top: Astaire with Dovima, one of photographer Richard Avedon's favorite models.
Bottom: Hepburn performs George Gershwin's "How Long Has This Been Going On?" in her first musical number.

"Friends, you saw enter here a waif, a gamin, a lowly caterpillar. We open the cocoon but it is not a butterfly that emerges. It is a bird of paradise."

—— Fashion designer Paul Duval (Robert Flemyng) on Jo's transformation from beatnik to model

LOVE IN THE AFTERNOON (1957)

ALLIED ARTISTS

DIRECTOR: BILLY WILDER

SCREENPLAY: BILLY WILDER AND I.A.L. DIAMOND

BASED ON THE NOVEL "ARIANE" BY CLAUDE ANET

PRINCIPAL CAST: GARY COOPER (FRANK FLANNAGAN), AUDREY HEPBURN (ARIANE CHAVASSE), MAURICE CHEVALIER (CLAUDE CHAVASSE) AND JOHN MCGIVER (MONSIEUR X)

Less than a week after wrapping *Funny Face*, Audrey Hepburn was back in front of the cameras for *Love in the Afternoon*. Reteaming with her *Sabrina* director, Billy Wilder, Hepburn began filming in Paris in July of 1956. At the time, her actor husband Mel Ferrer was shooting a film in the south of France. Although they met on the Riviera on weekends, Hepburn missed him terribly. It was not the happiest of times for her personally, but one would never know it, watching her sparkling performance in Wilder's adaptation of Claude Anet's novel *Ariane*.

Filmed on some of the most beautiful locations in Paris, *Love in the Afternoon* depicts a city that is in love with love. One of its citizens is an innocent cello student, Ariane Chavasse (Audrey Hepburn), who lives with her devoted father, Claude (Maurice Chevalier), a private detective. Although he tries to shield Ariane from the immoral, romantic activities that he routinely investigates,

Top: Ariane Chavasse (Hepburn), music conservatory student. Bottom: French screen legend Maurice Chevalier portrays Ariane's father, private detective Claude Chavasse.

Claude works in their apartment, which makes it easy for Ariane to pore over his files while he is away. One day, while watching her father develop pictures from his latest stakeout, Ariane gets her first look at Frank Flannagan (Gary Cooper), a notorious, globe-trotting millionaire playboy responsible for the breakup of many a marriage. When Ariane mentions that he is very attractive, Claude retorts that he is "very objectionable."

That same day, a client (John McGiver) comes in to see the evidence Claude has found on his suspected, philandering wife. When Claude hands over pictures of Flannagan with the client's wife, the client pulls out a gun and vows to shoot the millionaire lothario.

Eavesdropping on her father's meeting, Ariane decides to warn Flannagan. At the Ritz Hotel, she bursts into his suite to tell the startled millionaire and the client's wife that her husband is en route. While the woman hides, Ariane takes her place — to the surprise of her father's client, who apologizes and excuses himself.

Ariane sets out to leave as well, but Flannagan peppers her with questions. She tells him little — not even her name. Intrigued, Flannagan invites her to return. The next afternoon, in between sips of champagne and stolen kisses, Ariane listens to Flannagan's no-strings-attached philosophy on love and echoes his sentiments in a breezy manner. Believing he's found a kindred spirit, Flannagan suggests they get together again the next time he is in Paris.

Top: Ariane gets her first look at the "very objectionable" Mr. Flannagan. Bottom: Chavasse (Chevalier) hands over the evidence to a client (John McGiver).

After a year of pining for Flannagan, Ariane finally reunites with him. During their afternoons together, Ariane spins an outrageous tale of romantic conquests. Even though the men she mentions are from cases she read in her father's files, she confidently makes them her own. As he listens to Ariane, Flannagan finds himself increasingly uncomfortable with a heretofore unknown emotion: jealousy. Pushed to his limits, Flannagan decides to find out just who Ariane really is. It is an investigation that reveals romantic secrets and new possibilities.

At first glance, the premise of *Love in the Afternoon* — a virginal, young woman spins an elaborate yarn about her own romantic history to win the love of an aging ladies' man — seems to suggest an unsavory film. Indeed, the Catholic Legion of Decency threatened to place the film on its "Condemned List" until director Wilder agreed to add a voice-over that promised a wholesome outcome for the lovers.

One of three Wilder films released in 1957 (the others being *The Spirit of St. Louis* and *Witness for the Prosecution*), *Love in the Afternoon* pays elegant homage to the films of Wilder's idol/mentor, Ernst Lubitsch. Revered for "the Lubitsch

Ariane eavesdrops on a conversation between her father and a client.

"You know who I am, Mr. Flannagan, I'm the girl in the afternoon."

— Ariane (Hepburn)

touch" of sophistication and grace he brought to such classics as *Ninotchka* (1939) and *The Shop Around the Corner* (1940), Lubitsch hired Wilder to co-write the romantic comedy *Bluebeard's Eighth Wife* (1938), starring Gary Cooper and Claudette Colbert. *Love in the Afternoon* is more than a little reminiscent of Lubitsch's film, which casts Cooper as an American millionaire looking for his latest wife on the French Riviera. Of course, Cooper was all of 37 when he made *Bluebeard's Eighth Wife;* 19 years later, he looked all of his 56 years and older opposite the fresh-faced Hepburn.

Many critics at the time wrote that they believed Cooper was miscast and that the 28-year age difference between him and Hepburn was to the detriment of the film. Indeed some blamed the lackluster box office performance of the film upon this fact. However, the accent in this movie is not on exploring a physical relationship. As critic Alexander Walker noted in *Audrey: Her Real Story*, the strength of the movie is in seeing Hepburn's character bring out the better instincts of Cooper's character.

Hepburn gives another delightful performance. She deftly conveys an engaging combination of elegance and pluck that barely protects the vulnerable heart of her character, Ariane. Watching her listen carefully to Flannagan, echoing back his words and then weaving in the tales she absorbed from her father's files is a charming display of wit and savvy.

Audrey Hepburn enjoyed working with Gary Cooper, but apparently was not particularly fond of Maurice Chevalier. She found his form of flirtation a bit much. At one point she said,

Top: Ariane steps out on the Ritz Hotel window ledge to warn Mr. Flannagan. Bottom: American tycoon Frank Flannagan (Gary Cooper) questions Ariane about her own romantic life.

"It would have made more sense for Gary Cooper to have played my father and Chevalier my lover." Somehow, Wilder must have found a way to tame Chevalier. On film, Chevalier comes across as nothing but a loving father and one of the happiest of private detectives.

Love in the Afternoon marked the second and final collaboration between director Billy Wilder and Audrey Hepburn. While it never achieved the commercial and critical success of *Sabrina*, *Love in the Afternoon* did win its share of accolades. The film received three Golden Globe nominations in the categories of Best Motion Picture-Musical or Comedy, Best Actor-Musical or

"I know the rules. Love and run. Everybody's happy. Nobody gets hurt."

— Ariane (Hepburn)

Opposite page: Ariane spies on Flannagan at the opera. Top: The Gypsies play as Ariane models her ermine coat to Flannagan. Bottom: Ariane spins tall tales about her numerous lovers during a picnic.

Top: Flannagan and Ariane get cozy at the Ritz. Bottom: The beginning of the couple's May-December romance.

"They're very odd people, you know. When they're young, they have their teeth straightened, their tonsils taken out and gallons of vitamins pumped into them. Something happens to their insides! They become immunized, mechanized, air-conditioned and hydromatic."

— Ariane (Hepburn) about Americans

Comedy (Maurice Chevalier) and Best Actress-Musical or Comedy (Hepburn). The *New York Times* film critics named it one of the year's 10 best films, and it garnered an award for Best Screenplay-Comedy from the Writers Guild of America.

Ariane bids a tearful farewell to her lover.

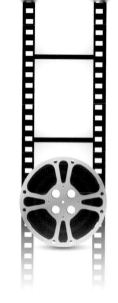

GREEN MANSIONS (1959)

MGM

DIRECTOR: MEL FERRER

SCREENPLAY: DOROTHY KINGSLEY

BASED ON THE NOVEL BY W. H. HUDSON

PRINCIPAL CAST: AUDREY HEPBURN (RIMA), ANTHONY PERKINS (ABEL), LEE J. COBB (NUFLO), SESSUE HAYAKAWA (RUNI) AND HENRY SILVA (KUA-KO)

Like every great artist, Audrey Hepburn longed to push herself creatively with work that would surprise her critics and fans. Toward the end of her first decade in front of the camera, she would test herself by taking a role once intended for Elizabeth Taylor: the ethereal heroine Rima of *Green Mansions*. In husband Mel Ferrer's pictorially beautiful but muddled adaptation of W. H. Hudson's 1904 novel, Hepburn would forego her beloved couture to wear one plain frock throughout the film, which Ferrer shot on location in South America and the MGM backlot.

Set in a remote South American jungle, where emotions are heightened by the pulse of the natural world and its ever-present dangers, *Green Mansions* follows the young adventurer Abel (Anthony Perkins) in his quest for legendary gold. When he encounters an aggressive tribe led by Chief Runi (silent screen star Sessue Hayakawa), Abel impresses them by standing his ground. Runi

Top: Rima (Hepburn) with Abel (Anthony Perkins), the young adventurer bewitched by the fabled "bird woman" of the jungle. Bottom: A fight to the death between the warrior Kua-Ko (Henry Silva) and Abel.

therefore decrees that this brave outsider must cross the river and kill the tribe's enemy: the deadly female spirit that dwells among the leaves.

As it turns out, this deadly female spirit is Rima (Hepburn), a gentle naïf who lives with her grandfather Nuflo (Lee J. Cobb) in a jungle compound — the green mansions of the title — communing with nature in an intuitive way. She floats though the trees, chirping to birds and trailed by a fawn; when Abel is bitten by a snake, she nurses him back to health with the same tenderness she lavishes on her animal friends. Yet once Nuflo realizes that his granddaughter is falling in love with the outsider, he drives Abel away, in a futile effort to protect Rima from the inevitable heartbreak. Abel soon returns, however, to protect Rima and Nuflo from the warrior Kua-Ko (Henry Silva), who's vowed to kill them. Leading them deeper into the jungle, Abel gradually learns the truth about Rima's past that her grandfather has long kept hidden.

For years, Hollywood filmmakers had tried to bring Hudson's romantic fable to the screen. In the 1930s, RKO bought the rights to make a film starring Dolores Del Rio, only to abandon the project. A decade later, MGM briefly considered making *Green Mansions* with Elizabeth Taylor, fresh off the success of *National Velvet* (1944), but it too was shelved. In 1954, director Vincente Minnelli went so far as to scout locations across South America for *his* version of *Green Mansions*, written by Broadway lyricist Alan Jay Lerner, and shoot a screen

Top: Nuflo (Lee J. Cobb) with his sheltered granddaughter. Bottom: Hepburn and Perkins on one of the film's elaborate jungle sets.

Mel Ferrer and Hepburn relax on the set of *Green Mansions*.

test of Italian actress Pier Angeli, who had posed as Rima for a *Life* magazine cover. Despite the time and money Minnelli spent on developing *Green Mansions*, longtime MGM producer Arthur Freed was underwhelmed by Angeli's screen test and vetoed the costly project. With the casting of Hepburn in *Green Mansions*, the search for the ideal actress to play Rima seemingly came to a happy end; hiring Ferrer to direct his wife would prove to be far more problematic.

Ferrer had been focused for many years on securing film deals, often on the strength of his wife's celebrity, while she often lived and worked in a different part of the world. Although he had previously directed a handful of films, including the well-received film noir *The Secret Fury* (1950), Ferrer had never tackled anything as ambitious as *Green Mansions*. To capture the natural splendor central to the story, Ferrer and his crew filmed in British Guiana, Columbia and Venezuela and returned with magnificent footage of jungles, rivers and waterfalls to use as background for the principal cast. He also hired the famed Brazilian composer Heitor Villa-Lobos to write the film's score, which Ferrer never used; Villa-Lobos later transformed his *Green Mansions* score into the symphonic poem, "Forest of the Amazon."

"Out here I believe in everything. Every leaf, every flower, birds, the air."

— Rima (Hepburn) to Abel (Perkins)

Unfortunately, Ferrer's autocratic personality, combined with his relative directorial inexperience, created a tense atmosphere on the MGM backlot, where much of the film was shot.

Many on the crew were particularly taken aback by Ferrer's attitude toward Hepburn, whom he treated like an assistant, rather than the film's star. As *Green Mansions*' production photographer Bob Willoughby recalled, "If the prop man forgot to bring Mel his morning orange juice, she brought it herself. In the afternoon she'd bring him tea and cookies." His sentiments were echoed by the film's choreographer Katherine Dunham, who said, "I felt [Ferrer] was not terribly sympathetic to her." For her part, Hepburn would later dismiss such criticisms of Ferrer: "Before we began, many friends asked me how such an artistically touchy situation would turn out.... I can say it was pleasantly uncomplicated. I found that being directed by Mel was as natural as brushing my teeth."

Yet the production of *Green Mansions* was nonetheless draining for Hepburn, who began shooting the film just weeks after completing *The Nun's Story,* which had been shot in the stifling heat of the Belgian Congo. She was also still recuperating from a severe case of kidney stones *and* had to pack and ship her personal possessions from Switzerland to Los Angeles, where she had not worked in five years. Whatever physical and emotional fatigue she was suffering during the film's production is not evident onscreen. Hepburn brings an angelic quality to the role that perfectly suits the mystical undercurrents to the film. Her eyes literally sparkle as Rima begins to experience her first feelings of romantic love; whispering her lines to Perkins, she seems to glow with serenity.

Hepburn's performance in *Green Mansions* was generally praised by critics, who were less than enchanted by Ferrer's filmmaking; *Variety*'s critic complained that the film's "fantastic elements puzzle and annoy," while the *New York Times'* Bosley Crowther dismissed *Green Mansions*' climax as "abrupt, melodramatic and contrived." Although MGM pulled out all the stops publicizing *Green Mansions,* it ultimately failed to resonate with audiences, even diehard Hepburn fans. While she would rebound with *The Nun's Story*, which premiered four months after *Green Mansions*, Ferrer would never direct another major motion picture.

"When I look at that hummingbird I see you. Standing still in the sunlight, then slipping away like a shadow."

— Abel (Perkins) to Rima (Hepburn)

"You've robbed her of her happiness, destroyed her peace of mind. What more do you want of her?!"

— Nuflo (Cobb) to Abel (Perkins)

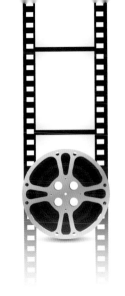

THE NUN'S STORY (1959)

WARNER BROTHERS PICTURES

DIRECTOR: FRED ZINNEMANN

SCREENPLAY: ROBERT ANDERSON

BASED ON THE BOOK BY KATHYRN C. HULME

PRINCIPAL CAST: AUDREY HEPBURN (SISTER LUKE/GABRIELLE VAN DER MAL), PETER FINCH (DR. FORTUNATI), DAME EDITH EVANS (MOTHER EMMANUEL), DAME PEGGY ASHCROFT (MOTHER MATHILDE), DEAN JAGGER (DR. VAN DER MAL), MILDRED DUNNOCK (SISTER MARGHARITA), BEATRICE STRAIGHT (MOTHER CHRISTOPHE) AND PATRICIA COLLINGE (SISTER WILLIAM)

She had played a runaway princess in *Roman Holiday* (1953), a Tolstoy heroine in *War and Peace* (1956) and a high-fashion model in *Funny Face* (1957), but when Audrey Hepburn agreed to star in Academy Award-winning director Fred Zinnemann's *The Nun's Story*, she undertook what is perhaps the most demanding role of her career.

As the idealistic Belgian girl Gabrielle Van der Mal, later to become the dedicated and devout Sister Luke, torn between the rules of the cloistered Order to which she has pledged herself and her own conscience, Hepburn is quietly magnificent. In one of the greatest matches of actor and role in the history of movies (the part was first offered to Ingrid Bergman who turned it down, suggesting they offer it to Hepburn) the actress fuses her already established screen persona of purity and innocence with an unmatched empathy for the inner life of its lead character. The critic Stanley Kauffmann wrote: "Audrey Hepburn's performance as Sister Luke is better than her sheer ability could make it, because her person is

Top: The postulant Gabrielle van der Mal (Hepburn).
Bottom: Brides of Christ.

so right for the part. After she has done all she can do with knowledge, her beauty speaks for her. Hepburn's beauty serves as an intensifying glass for the inner travail she is trying to convey." Indeed, Hepburn profoundly demonstrates the depths of her acting ability in *The Nun's Story*, forever obliterating criticisms that she was just a "model." Through stillness, silence and the use of her eyes, she creates one of her most memorable, complex and transcendent screen characters.

Playwright Robert Anderson's stellar adaptation of Kathryn C. Hulme's 1956 nonfiction bestseller depicts the religious way of life with an unflinching honesty rarely, if ever, seen in the films of Hollywood's golden era. The cloistered, convent life of 1920s-era Bruges, Belgium, provides the backdrop for *The Nun's Story*, which follows Gabrielle (Hepburn) as she leaves behind her worldly possessions, bids farewell to her family and friends and enters the convent to begin her life as a nun. Despite the misgivings of her famous surgeon father, Dr. Van der Mal (Dean Jagger, in a moving performance), Gabrielle is certain of her religious vocation and determined to succeed. As she learns to be a "good nun," Gaby is immediately confronted with her character "imperfections." Most striking is her inability to obey the convent rules unconditionally. But she perseveres and eventually takes her final vows. Known as Sister Luke, she commits to a life of poverty, chastity and obedience until death.

After a series of grueling tests — including a harrowing brush with death involving a schizophrenic

Top: Gabrielle takes her first vows and receives the name of Sister Luke. Bottom: Sister Luke learns she will attend the school of tropical medicine in Antwerp.

patient (Colleen Dewhurst) at a convent-run mental sanitarium — Sister Luke is sent to the Congo as a nursing nun. Her dreams of treating the natives are quickly dashed, however, when she learns she can only treat European patients at a Congo hospital. And working alongside the handsome atheist Dr. Fortunati (Peter Finch) only compounds Sister Luke's ongoing struggle to overcome pride.

When a nurse is needed to accompany an important person in need of emergency medical care to Belgium, Sister Luke must leave the Congo and return to convent life, where she is to serve as a "good example" to the other nuns. Unable to return to the Congo due to the outbreak of World War II, Sister Luke continues to wrestle with her doubts after the Nazis invade Belgium. Expected to feel love toward the Nazi occupiers, Sister Luke experiences a crisis of faith that ultimately forces her to make a life-changing decision.

Hepburn's preparation for *The Nun's Story* exceeded anything she had done for her earlier roles. She observed convent life inside a French convent, visited

Sister Luke receives some disappointing news in the Congo.

"You can cheat your sisters, but you cannot cheat yourself or God."

— Sister Luke (Hepburn)

both an insane asylum and a leper colony, talked to missionary workers and watched surgical procedures. She also endured a marathon 132-day, globe-trotting shoot and suffered an excruciating bout with kidney stones, due in part to the dehydration she endured in the Congo, where temperatures reached upwards of 130 degrees. Yet she remained unfailingly gracious and bore the hardship stoically, according to Zinnemann, who later marveled at her lack of movie star pretense: "There was no ego.... There was the greatest consideration for her co-workers."

Hepburn also formed a lifelong friendship with the real-life Sister Luke, Marie-Louise Habets, whom Hepburn consulted on every detail of her character. In fact, the two women, along with *The Nun's Story* author Kathryn C. Hulme, became so close that people christened them "The 3-H Club."

Although Hepburn appears in virtually every scene, she manages the difficult feat of holding the viewer's gaze without overshadowing the superb character actresses playing nuns, most notably Dame Edith Evans as Mother Emanuel and Academy Award winners Dame Peggy Ashcroft (*A Passage to India*) and Beatrice Straight (*Network*) as Mother Mathilde and Mother Christophe, respectively. Hepburn also does some of her best screen acting opposite Finch in scenes laced with palpable sexual tension, and bravely holds her own opposite Dewhurst in the brutal asylum fight scene. Refusing a stunt double, Hepburn instead learned how to wrestle in a full nun's garb without tearing a ligament.

Top: Sister Luke confesses to Mother Mathilde (Peggy Ashcroft) that she's failed another test of obedience. Bottom: Sister Luke meets Father Vermeuhlen (Niall MacGinnis) during her visit to a leper colony in the Congo.

"…any resemblance between the present Hepburn and the former one dating back to January 1st of 1958 (before filming of *The Nun's Story* began) is purely accidental. I have seen, heard, learnt so much and have been so enriched by a milliard experiences that I am and feel a different person.… Delving into the heart and mind of Sister Luke, I have also had to dig deep down in myself…and I hope (this) will result in harvesting a better Audrey."

— Hepburn

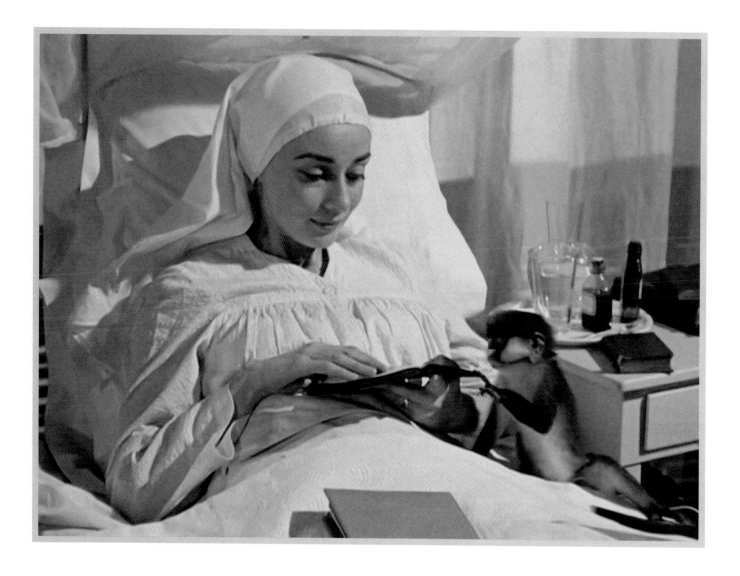

A surprise box office smash that became Warner Bros. Pictures' top grossing film to date, *The Nun's Story* was an across-the-board triumph for the film's cast and crew. It received eight Academy Award nominations, including Best Picture, Best Director and Best Actress; and the Motion Picture Academy recognized Franz Waxman's beautiful score (his 11th of 12th nominations!) and Franz Planer's stunning cinematography. It was the second film for Planer and Hepburn, who had previously worked together on *Roman Holiday*. They would reteam for three more films: *The Unforgiven* (1960), *Breakfast at Tiffany's* (1961) and *The Children's Hour* (1962).

Opposite page top: Sister Luke at a psychic crossroads. Opposite page Bottom: The quietly powerful final shot of *The Nun's Story*. Top: Sister Luke recuperates from tuberculosis with the help of a little friend.

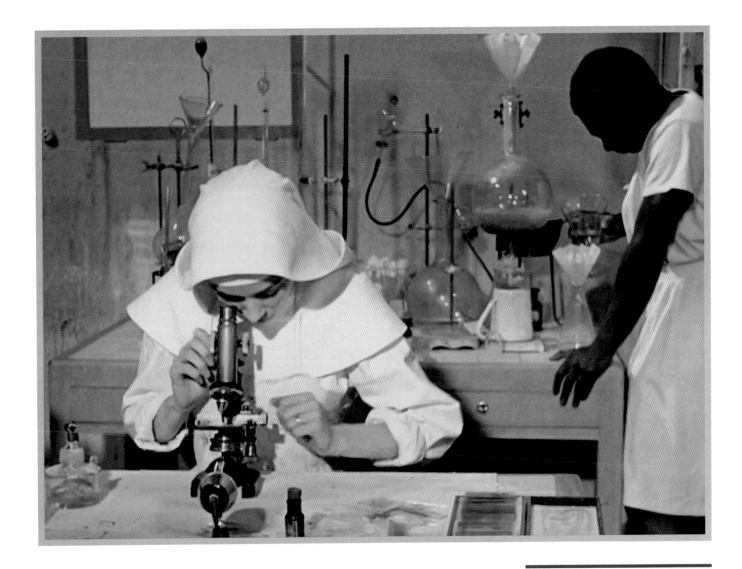

Shut out at the Oscar race, *The Nun's Story* nevertheless earned Hepburn the Best Actress prize from both the New York Film Critics and the British Academy Awards. More importantly, it forever erased any doubts about Hepburn's dramatic range. In the words of the critic for *Films in Review*, "Her portrayal of Sister Luke is one of the great performances of the screen."

"A soaring and luminous film (in which) Audrey Hepburn has her most demanding film and gives her finest performance."

— *Variety* on *The Nun's Story*

Opposite page: Sister Luke at work in the Congo hospital. Top: Australian actor Peter Finch gives a passionate performance as the dedicated physician, Dr. Fortunati. Bottom: Acclaimed stage actress Colleen Dewhurst as the schizophrenic "Gabriel."

"The most gripping and dramatic personal story of this decade is on the screen!"

— *The Nun's Story* tagline

PART 3

1960-1967

UDREY HEPBURN: 1960-1967

The world of the 1960s seemed to grow younger and more rebellious — in everything from its fashion to its politics — but Hepburn was maturing into the only roles she ever really wanted to play: wife and mother. One might have foreseen her eventual if temporary — departure from show business after 1967. But only those closest to her ght have foreseen the dissolution of her marriage to Mel Ferrer in 1968.

By 1960, Hepburn was in her thirties, and she gave birth to her first son, Sean, after oduction on *The Unforgiven* had wrapped. Two prior miscarriages had plunged her into ep depression. Now, Sean was the miracle she had been desperate for, and he became the nter of her world. She found herself choosing her film roles less for their inherent worth d more for logistical reasons: i.e., would they allow her to stay close to home? She entered o temporary semi-retirements, rejecting more film roles than she accepted, including es in *A Taste of Honey* (1961) and *In the Cool of the Day* (1963).

HEPBURN'S LEADING MEN, 1960-1967

RT FINNEY
r the Road (1967)

ears after achieving international m with his Academy Award–nomi- performance as *Tom Jones* (1963), tish stage actor made one of his ient screen appearances opposite rn in this bittersweet portrait of a ge on the rocks. The burly actor ailed as a "second Olivier" would quently earn four more Academy nominations for his performances der on the Orient Express* (1974), resser* (1983), *Under the Volcano*

CARY GRANT
Charade (1963)

Hands down, the most debonair and suavely handsome of Hollywood's great stars, Grant is the perfect screen partner for Hepburn in *Charade*. The stars launch a major charm offensive in Stanley Donen's marvelous comic thriller, one of the last films Grant made before retiring from acting in 1966. Equally at home in screwball comedies and Alfred Hitchcock thrillers, Grant had earlier turned down roles opposite Hepburn in *Sabrina* (1954) and *Love in the Afternoon* (1957).

REX HARRISON
My Fair Lady (1964)

Nicknamed "Sexy Rexy" by columnist Walter Winchell, the British stage actor achieved his greatest fame as Professor Henry Higgins, the linguistics expert playing Pygmalion to Eliza Doolittle's Galatea in *My Fair Lady* (1964 Although he had reportedly treated Julie Andrews with utmost contempt during the original Broadway run of the Lerner and Loewe musical, Harrison was besotted with Hepburn, whom he called h favorite leading lady." The Oscar winner would

The roles she did accept, however, often created scandal or controversy. She was not the first or most obvious choice for the two roles for which she is perhaps best known — Holly Golightly in *Breakfast at Tiffany's* (1961) and Eliza Doolittle in *My Fair Lady* (1964). Other roles, like Karen Wright in *The Children's Hour* (1961), which took advantage of the Production Code's crumbling authority, often challenged traditional mores and values — to both plaudits and brickbat reviews.

But Hepburn's circle of friends and admirers was expanding. In 1963, she sang "Happy Birthday" to President John F. Kennedy, managing to create far less fuss and controversy with her simple rendition than Marilyn Monroe had with hers the year before. Unfortunately, that November, during production of *My Fair Lady*, Hepburn also had the unhappy task of announcing his death to the crew.

In the meantime, she had befriended actress Deborah Kerr, best known for roles in *From Here to Eternity* (1953) and *The King and I* (1956). Though the two often went months without seeing each other, they remained close friends, and

BURT LANCASTER
The Unforgiven (1960)

A truly larger-than-life figure, acrobat-turned-actor Lancaster gives a powerful performance as Hepburn's adoptive brother in John Huston's western. Nineteen sixty would turn out to be a banner year for Lancaster, who won the Best Actor Academy Award for his mesmerizing performance of the title role in *Elmer Gantry* (1960), Richard Brooks' adaptation of Sinclair Lewis' 1927 novel about a sham evangelist. Two years later, Lancaster would receive the third of his four Academy Award nominations of a

PETER O'TOOLE
How to Steal a Million (1966)

The most nominated actor to never win the Academy Award, eight-time Oscar bridesmaid O'Toole shows off his comic flair as Hepburn's accomplice in William Wyler's lighthearted heist film. The preternaturally handsome British actor with the commanding voice received his greatest acclaim for his starring roles in *Lawrence of Arabia* (1962), *Becket* (1964) and *The Lion in Winter* (1968). In 2003, the Motion Picture Academy presented O'Toole with an honorary Academy Award for his body of work.

GEORGE PEPPARD
Breakfast at Tiffany's (1961)

Despite leading roles in such films as *How the West Was One* (1962) and *The Blue Max* (1966), superstardom eluded Peppard, who had first attracted attention playing Robert Mitchum's illegitimate son in *Home from the Hill* (1960). Although he shines as Hepburn's love interest in *Breakfast at Tiffany's*, Peppard alienated cast and crew with his egotistical behavior off-camera. While he worked steadily in film until 1992, Peppard achieved his biggest success as the star of the 1980s television series *The*

Kerr spoke of her fondly. Hepburn's agent Kurt Frings had also been instrumental in encouraging a friendship between the Ferrers and Elizabeth Taylor and Eddie Fisher. Mel Ferrer and Fisher perhaps bonded over the fact that their respective wives were more famous than they. Hepburn and Taylor — who had just won the Academy Award for *Butterfield 8* (1960) — remained friends for life.

Though Hepburn always strove to be unerringly generous and thoughtful in her personal relationships, she could not avoid public scrutiny and scandal entirely. At the 1965 Academy Awards ceremony, she was criticized for appearing to snub Patricia Neal, who was to have presented the Best Actor award that night but had suffered a minor stroke. When Hepburn was asked to fill in, she failed to mention Neal — at all. Neal's husband, author Roald Dahl, was outraged, and the press was quick to pounce on the faux pas.

By 1967, Hepburn, who had always been paired with older men on-screen, had finally been cast with two male co-stars closer to her own age: Peter O'Toole (in *How to Steal a Million*) and Albert Finney (in *Two For the Road*). Those friendships gave her a new *joie de vive* and a sense of independence outside Mel's watchful eye. They may well have signaled the beginning of the end of the marriage she had worked so hard to maintain.

"I don't want to be a perennial teenager."

— Hepburn

Opposite page: Hepburn in *Wait Until Dark* (1967). Top: Hepburn and Peppard in *Breakfast at Tiffany's* (1961).

More importantly, Hollywood and the film industry at large were undergoing a sea change. Box office attendance had declined dramatically. Competition from both television and overseas films, as well as rising costs, forced studios to cut back on film production. The studio system was crumbling. Stars who had been tied to studio contracts now found themselves free agents, and many started their own independent production companies. The studios, in turn, often gambled on gimmicks like Smell-o-Vision or lavish, widescreen epics to lure audiences back, but more often than not, they lost to upstart rivals who catered to that newly expanding and lucrative demographic: youth.

After having made a name for herself as the wispy novice, Hepburn had matured over time into more adult roles. But after she and Ferrer divorced in 1968, Hepburn decided to leave Hollywood behind and focus once again on motherhood.

THE UNFORGIVEN (1960)

UNITED ARTISTS

DIRECTOR: JOHN HUSTON

SCREENPLAY: BEN MADDOW

BASED ON THE NOVEL BY ALAN LEMAY

PRINCIPAL CAST: BURT LANCASTER (BEN ZACHARY), AUDREY HEPBURN (RACHEL ZACHARY), AUDIE MURPHY (CASH ZACHARY), LILLIAN GISH (MATILDA ZACHARY), JOHN SAXON (JOHNNY PORTUGAL), DOUG MCCLURE (ANDY ZACHARY) AND CHARLES BICKFORD (ZEB RAWLINS)

If fans of the elegant gamine Audrey Hepburn were happily surprised by her dramatic turn as a nun in *The Nun's Story* (1959), they were certainly taken aback by her next film role in *The Unforgiven*, where she plays a prairie girl who shoos away a cow and uses the word *ain't* in the first spoken lines of the film's opening scene. This line is one of many memorable ones in an unusually affecting and powerfully acted film, skillfully directed by two-time Academy Award winner John Huston.

Based on Alan LeMay's novel, *The Unforgiven* resembles John Ford's *The Searchers* (1956) — another adaptation of a LeMay novel — in its depiction of racism in the 19th-century American West. The story centers on the Zachary clan, a frontier family in Texas of the 1860s headed by oldest son Ben (Burt Lancaster). When a mysterious stranger reveals that the family's adopted daughter Rachel (Hepburn) may have been stolen from the local Kiowa tribe, the Zacharys' ranch-partner neighbors turn against

Top: Hepburn goes rustic in *The Unforgiven*, her only western. Bottom: Hepburn gives one of her most underrated performances as Rachel Zachary in John Huston's *The Unforgiven*.

them, as tensions escalate into a violent showdown.

Filmed on location in Durango, Mexico, *The Unforgiven* was plagued with problems from the first day of shooting. While Huston had wanted the film to make a "statement" about racism and intolerance, star Burt Lancaster, screenwriter Ben Maddow (who had previously written *The Asphalt Jungle* for Huston) and studio United Artists were primarily interested in creating a box office blockbuster. The matter only came to a head once shooting began. Years later, Huston felt he had sold out by compromising on that point. From then on, he later said, "Everything went to hell."

Huston wasn't exaggerating. Hepburn's co-star Audie Murphy almost drowned in a boating accident on location. Calamity also befell Hepburn, a novice horseback rider, who was thrown by a white Arabian stallion and fractured four vertebrae and tore her lower back muscles. Before fainting, she had whispered to Lancaster, "I had to do something to get out of this hell hole." Hepburn's recovery delayed production by more than a month. In an amazing bit of irony, she was nursed back to health by the woman she had just portrayed in *The Nun's Story*, Marie-Louise Habets (or "Sister Lou," as Hepburn called her). Ever the trouper, Hepburn literally "got back on the horse" when she returned to Durango, where she shot the scene without incident this time (the horse had been sedated to ensure docility).

Hepburn's monthlong convalescence proved

Top: Rachel questions her mother Matilda (Lillian Gish) about an encounter with a mysterious visitor. Bottom: Silent screen star Lillian Gish surprised Huston and star Burt Lancaster with her shooting skills.

Rachel with her brother Cash (Audie Murphy). World War II's most decorated soldier, Murphy enjoyed modest success as a film and television actor.

costly for the already big-budgeted western. According to Huston, Lancaster's and Hepburn's salaries exceeded the final budget for his film noir classic, *The Maltese Falcon* (1941). One of the film's sets, an authentic replica of a pioneer sod house — specially designed in fitted segments by art director Stephen B. Grimes so that it could be taken apart for varied reverse-angle shots — cost $300,000 to construct! Each day's footage was flown to London for processing and then flown back to Mexico for Huston to edit. All told, the final cost for *The Unforgiven* ran to $6 million (an enormous sum in those days).

Fortunately, all of the money shows up on the screen. *The Unforgiven* is a big, old-fashioned epic, with the sweep and emotional heft of the classic westerns. Cinematographer Franz Planer captures stunning images of the flat, sun-bleached ranch the Zacharys call home. Huston expertly stages both the film's action sequences and the more intimate moments of family strife. And four-time Academy Award–winning composer Dimitri Tiomkin contributes one of his most passionate and eclectic film scores, with its snatches from the

"Shoo, now. Shoo! Ain't you got no better manners than to eat at the top of a house."

— Rachel (Hepburn) addressing a cow eating atop her house

works of Charles Berlioz, Anton Bruckner and Gustav Mahler.

Huston also draws unusually fine performances from his entire cast. As the eldest Zachary brother in love with his adopted Kiowa sister, Lancaster is a bold, magnetic presence. He and Hepburn receive sterling support from silent screen legend Lillian Gish as Matilda, the Zachary matriarch; in one of *The Unforgiven*'s most arresting scenes, the diminutive actress attacks a horse carrying a lynching victim. And real-life World War II hero Murphy — who had previously played himself in *To Hell and Back* (1955) — recovered from his near-drowning to give a strong performance as Cash Zachary, the racist middle brother who turns on Rachel and nearly abandons the family. Although he would continue making films until 1969, *The Unforgiven* would turn out to be Murphy's last major studio film.

As Rachel, Hepburn gives a quiet, resolute performance that radiates inner strength. As co-star Doug McClure (who plays her youngest brother in the film) noted, she does some wonderful internal things in her performance. Yet her performance was initially dismissed by most critics. In fact, *The New Republic*'s Stanley Kauffman pronounced it "bad." Even fervent Hepburn admirer Bosley Crowther of the *New York Times* found her "a bit too polished, too fragile and civilized" to portray a Kiowa woman in the 1860s-era Texas Panhandle convincingly.

Like Hepburn, *The Unforgiven* received generally negative reviews. Huston himself would later disown the film, calling it "bombastic and overinflated. Everything in it is bigger than life." But this is an example where a director can be

Top: Ben Zachary (Burt Lancaster) takes his adopted sister Rachel for a ride. Bottom: A tense moment at the Zachary family table.

> "So many wonderful things were going on inside her…she played it very realistically…those eyes!"
>
> — Co-star Doug McClure on working with and being mesmerized by Hepburn in *The Unforgiven*

Top: Veteran character actor Charles Bickford as ranch owner Zeb Rawlins. Bottom: One of cinematographer Franz F. Planer's striking vistas in *The Unforgiven*. Opposite page: Rachel is crisis.

wrong about one of his own films. Admittedly, there are moments when the film nearly descends into histrionics, but *The Unforgiven* remains a highly absorbing and unusual western, with a strong undercurrent of mysticism.

Whatever its shortcomings, *The Unforgiven* is a near-great film that deserves reappraisal — as does Hepburn's performance. Perhaps Huston was closer to the mark than he realized when he said about his star's performance at the time the film was made: "She's as good as the other Hepburn."

"She's as good as the other Hepburn."

— John Huston, director of *The Unforgiven* on Hepburn's performance

"Audrey Hepburn gives a shining performance as the foundling daughter of a frontier family."

— *Variety* review

"Have you read any good stories lately with a small part in it for a girl who's good at falling off horses?"

— note from Hepburn to director John Huston, after her horseback riding accident

"A Texas-sized package bursting with action, mystery and romance!"

— *The Hollywood Reporter*

Opposite page: Audie Murphy and Burt Lancaster as brothers whose relationship turns volatile in *The Unforgiven*. Top: Rachel struggles to accept the truth about her mixed-race heritage. Bottom: Lancaster and Hepburn share a rare lighthearted moment in *The Unforgiven*.

"A new triumph from Academy Award winner John Huston"

– *The Unforgiven* tagline

BREAKFAST AT TIFFANY'S (1961)

PARAMOUNT PICTURES

DIRECTOR: BLAKE EDWARDS

SCREENPLAY: GEORGE AXELROD

BASED ON THE NOVELLA BY TRUMAN CAPOTE

PRINCIPAL CAST: AUDREY HEPBURN (HOLLY GOLIGHTLY), GEORGE PEPPARD (PAUL VARJAK), PATRICIA NEAL (MRS. FALENSON/ 2E), BUDDY EBSEN (DOC GOLIGHTLY), MARTIN BALSAM (O.J. BERMAN) VILALLONGA (JOSE DE SILVA PERREIRA) AND MICKEY ROONEY (MR. YUNIOSHI)

That black dress and pearls, that cigarette holder, those Ray-Ban Wayfarer sunglasses — these are the iconic fashion essentials of Hepburn's most beloved character, Manhattan party girl Holly Golightly. Women have tried to emulate the style and sophisticated charm of the *Breakfast at Tiffany's* heroine for decades. The "little black dress" Holly tosses on to visit her mobster patron in prison is a staple in many a woman's closet. Producer Richard Shepherd recalled that after the movie was released, he saw versions of Holly's purse everywhere he went. However, it takes more than great fashion sense to make a film a classic; it takes an incandescent performance by a Hollywood star of the first magnitude.

Holly Golightly is a young woman of pure invention who carries herself as a sophisticated, cosmopolitan socialite. The fact that she accepts money from her various dates does not seem to damper her spirits or trouble her conscience. Staying out all night, sprinkling her speech with French phrases, and wearing stylish clothing, Holly

Top: Hepburn in the film's classic opening scene.
Bottom: The sleepy, but always stylish Holly Golightly (Hepburn) answers the door.

charms her way through her life in pursuit of the richest sugar daddy she can find — even though she considers most men "rats."

Holly's life forever changes when a young writer, Paul Varjak (George Peppard), moves into her building. Although he's published a book of short stories, Paul is now living like Holly; he's basically the "kept man" of a rich society matron (Patricia Neal). From this common ground, Holly and Paul build a friendship that eventually develops into the very last thing Holly wants: a romance with a penniless writer who sees the pain and loneliness she conceals beneath her party girl façade.

Audrey Hepburn is so deeply associated with the role of Holly Golightly that it is difficult to imagine anyone else in the role, but she was not the first actress considered. Truman Capote, the writer of the *Breakfast of Tiffany's* novella, wanted Marilyn Monroe to play Holly Golightly. In his version of the story, Holly lives a harsher reality and Monroe seemed like the perfect actress for the role. As Capote later told an interviewer for *Playgirl* magazine, "Holly had to have something touching about her … unfinished. Marilyn had that."

Breakfast at Tiffany's producers Richard Shepherd and Martin Jurow did not share Capote's enthusiasm for Monroe, whom they dismissed as "kind of obvious for the part."

They wanted someone who was "emotionally vulnerable and sensitive" and could reveal the

Top: Paul (George Peppard) watches Holly get ready for a visit to Sing Sing prison. Bottom: Hepburn at her most chic.

character's underlying sadness. In short, they wanted Audrey Hepburn. Hepburn owed Paramount Pictures another movie, but studio executives believed she would never do the film, since the character was a 180-degree departure from the guileless ingénues she had played in such films as *Roman Holiday* (1953) and *Sabrina* (1954). To Paramount Pictures' surprise, Hepburn signed on for *Breakfast at Tiffany's*.

Nor was director Blake Edwards the first choice for the film either. Shepherd and Jurow were originally considering John Frankenheimer, but they quickly dismissed him since his vision for the film seemed too dark. Edwards, on the other hand, saw the film as an effervescent comedy, as light and bubbly as Dom Pérignon. The memorable wild party scene at Holly's apartment is essentially his invention. When it was shot, Edwards ordered up cases of champagne and invited the assembled actors to improvise. Blending and building his own ideas off the actors' improvisations, Edwards created a lively scene full of clever slapstick and sight gags.

Holly shows Paul how to hail a cab.

"It's useful being top banana in the shock department."

— Holly (Hepburn)

After a short, initial rough patch of miscommunication, Blake Edwards and Audrey Hepburn enjoyed a happy and productive collaboration. Edwards later commented that Hepburn brought so much of her own charm to the role that he was convinced many filmgoers watched the entirety of *Breakfast at Tiffany's* without ever really grasping what Holly did to pay the rent.

Edwards was not as pleased with George Peppard, then being touted as another James Dean. While they got along on a personal level, Edwards admits, "I didn't want him in the movie.... He just didn't have whatever it was that I wanted." Actress Patricia Neal, who knew Peppard from the Actor's Studio, was not a fan either. She felt "he had been spoiled" and that his own vanity got in the way of his performance.

The most controversial casting choice in *Breakfast at Tiffany's* was Mickey Rooney for the part of Mr. Yunioshi, Holly Golightly's cantankerous Japanese neighbor. At the time, producer Richard Shepherd believed Rooney was a fine actor, but had reservations about a Caucasian actor playing a Japanese character. Unfortunately, Edwards didn't share Shepherd's concern and directed Rooney to portray Yunioshi as a broad ethnic stereotype — a directorial choice he came to regret, as he later admitted: "I didn't really think it out.... Looking back, I wish I had never done it."

Whatever casting mistakes may have been made in *Breakfast at Tiffany's*, they were readily forgiven by audiences, who embraced the film, turning it into a box office hit. Critics, on the other hand, were less enchanted with the creative

Top: Holly gets a bead on Paul's relationship with his "decorator" (Patricia Neal). Bottom: Drunken Mag Wildwood (Dorothy Whitney) tweaks the nose of millionaire Rusty Trawler (Stanley Adams) at Holly's riotous party.

liberties Edwards and screenwriter George Axelrod took with Capote's novella. Influential film critic Pauline Kael wrote, "If you've read the Truman Capote novella that the movie is based on (and even if you haven't) you may be dismayed to see things go soft and romantic." *Variety* called the screenplay "whitewashed." As for Capote, he disparaged it as "a mawkish valentine…. It bore as much resemblance to my work as the Rockettes do to Ulanova."

In contrast, the reviews for Hepburn were mostly glowing. In the *New York Times*, A.H. Weiler raved, "Above all, it has the overpowering attribute known as

"She's a crazy and a phony, but she's a real phony. Know what I mean, kid?"

— O.J. Berman (Martin Balsam)

Opposite page: Holly sings "Moon River," which was nearly cut from the film. Top: Doc (Buddy Ebsen) asks Paul to do him a favor. Bottom: Mickey Rooney as Holly's neighbor Mr. Yunioshi — an embarrassing example of Hollywood perpetuating crude racial stereotypes.

Audrey Hepburn." She would receive her fourth Best Actress Academy Award nomination for *Breakfast at Tiffany's*, losing to Sophia Loren for *Two Women*. Only *Breakfast at Tiffany's* composer Henry Mancini emerged victorious at the Oscars, winning two statuettes for Best Score and Best Original Song for "Moon River," co-written with lyricist Johnny Mercer.

Now regarded as one of the greatest songs ever written for American film, "Moon River" almost didn't make it into the final cut of *Breakfast at Tiffany's*. Paramount executives wanted to get rid of it after previewing the film in San Francisco. In a story that's become Hollywood legend, Hepburn reportedly leapt from her chair and declared "Over my dead body!" Happily for all involved, Hepburn prevailed.

"She was some kind of spectacular lady."

— Director Blake Edwards on Hepburn

Opposite page: Paul and Holly spend a romantic day together in New York. Top: A Tiffany's salesman (John McGiver) comes to the assistance of Holly and Paul. Bottom: Paul and Holly's first kiss.

THE CHILDREN'S HOUR (1961)

UNITED ARTISTS

DIRECTED BY: WILLIAM WYLER

SCREENPLAY: JOHN MICHAEL HAYES

BASED ON LILLIAN HELLMAN'S ADAPTATION OF HER PLAY

PRINCIPAL CAST: AUDREY HEPBURN (KAREN WRIGHT), SHIRLEY MACLAINE (MARTHA DOBIE), JAMES GARNER (DR. JOE CARDIN), MIRIAM HOPKINS (MRS. LILY MORTAR), FAY BAINTER (MRS. AMELIA TILFORD), KAREN BALKIN (MARY TILFORD) AND VERONICA CARTWRIGHT (ROSALIE WELLS)

The second of Hepburn's three films with director William Wyler, *The Children's Hour* seems to balance on a tipping point for both Hepburn's career and for Hollywood. Her last black-and-white film, it both obeyed and challenged the Motion Picture Production Code, and offered Hepburn an opportunity to graduate from "princess" fare like *Roman Holiday* (1953) to more mature, challenging material. As headmistress Karen Wright, Hepburn displays all the characteristic warmth, charm and grace audiences would come to expect, but showcases something extra: a kind of steely but elegant strength, an intelligence that commands respect.

Based on the 1934 play by Lillian Hellman, and on Hellman's own adaptation of the material, *The Children's Hour* centers around the exclusive "Wright-Dobie School for Girls," run by longtime friends Karen Wright and Martha Dobie (Shirley MacLaine). The film opens on a seemingly idyllic world: a relatively small school in the

Top: Headmistresses Martha Dobie (Shirley MacLaine) and Karen Wright (Hepburn) congratulate each other on their successful girls' school. Bottom: James Garner co-stars as Hepburn's fiancé, the supportive but impatient-to-marry Dr. Joe Cardin.

country, where girls can ride bikes, play by the lake, give piano recitals and learn elocution. By all accounts, the school seems to be doing well; Martha tells Karen they are even $90 ahead for the month. The women face two dilemmas, however: Karen's fiancé, Joe Cardin (James Garner), is pressuring her to get married and settle down; and 12-year-old Mary Tilford (Karen Balkin), the granddaughter of the school's wealthiest patron, has become the school's own answer to *The Bad Seed*. Mary is a pathological liar who suffers no compunction about blackmailing fellow students, corrupting them with illicit reading materials, or forcing them to accept blame for her own misdeeds.

When Karen attempts to discipline Mary for one minor lie, Mary retaliates with an even more grandiose fabrication. It begins as Mary's classmates eavesdrop on an argument between Martha and her meddlesome Aunt Lily Mortar (Miriam Hopkins, who played Martha in Wyler's 1936 film version of Hellman's play, *These Three*). Mary pieces together that gossip with the half-truths she gathers while spying on the headmistresses, and tattles the whole sordid tale to her grandmother, Amelia Tilford (Fay Bainter).

Martha is accused of nursing a possessive and "unnatural" affection for Karen. Whether the garrulous Aunt Lily or the prepubescent Mary fully understand the implications of the charge is a matter left to the viewer's own judgment, but it becomes evident that Amelia understands the subtext all too well. She swiftly

Top: The devious Mary (Karen Balkin) spies on Karen after hours. Bottom: Karen Balkin portrays Mary, the agent of the women's downfall in *The Children's Hour*.

embarks on a whisper campaign of slander, and soon the entire town has removed every child from the school. In the wake of such disaster, the two women and Joe are left to ferret out the truth, face being made the objects of public spectacle and ridicule, and confront the true state of their relationships.

Upon its release, the film received lukewarm or dismissive reviews. The *New York Times'* Bosley Crowther even likened the film's treatment of such sensitive issues to "some dotty old doll in bombazine with her mouth sagging open in shocked amazement" and sums up with: "there is nothing about this picture of which [director William Wyler] can be very proud." Only Hepburn was spared Crowther's vitriol; in his otherwise scathing review, he wrote that she "gives the impression of being sensitive and pure."

If websites such as IMDb or Turner Classic Movies are any indication, however, contemporary audiences appear to treat the film more kindly. While some regard it as so much ham-fisted soap opera, most applaud the performances and express appreciation for the film's willingness to tackle a taboo subject like homosexuality.

Karen Wright knows a lie when she hears one.

"Child, love, friend, woman — every word has a new meaning…"

— Karen Wright (Hepburn)

In fact, any overt expression of homo-sexuality had been strictly forbidden by the Motion Picture Production Code, which began officially policing the film industry for morally objectionable content in 1934. When Wyler and Hellman first adapted *The Children's Hour* for the screen in 1936, they deleted any references to lesbianism from the film, retitled *These Three*. Schoolgirl Mary Tilford instead spreads a lie that Martha spent the night with Karen's fiancé.

Though it wasn't phased out in favor of the MPAA rating system until 1968, the force of the Code began to weaken in the late 1950s and early 1960s, as more risqué foreign and Hollywood fare were proving to be box office hits, even without the Code's Seal of Approval. This relaxation of standards allowed Wyler to create a more faithful and forthright adaptation of Hellman's play, but the Code still required him to make certain concessions. He cut several scenes alluding to Martha's sexuality from the finished film and portrayed Martha as a guilt-ridden and self-loathing young woman. The film could portray a lesbian, so long as the word was never spoken and so long as she acknowledged her "moral decay."

Later on, Shirley MacLaine admitted that the cast never discussed the ramifications of the story they were telling. She and Hepburn entered the project with a kind of innocence, never questioning the characters' motives or choices, "not really understanding what we were basically doing." Now MacLaine believes that Martha would fight for her "budding preference" and that anything short would cause a "tremendous outcry."

Top: Martha argues with meddling Aunt Lily, played by Miriam Hopkins, who played MacLaine's role in the 1936 version *These Three*. Bottom: Hepburn radiates strength and warmth in the role of Karen Wright.

While much of the film would seem to belong to MacLaine and her brave performance, Hepburn distinguishes herself with a kind of reserve. Where her co-stars are fiery and tempestuous, she is measured. Where they pace and gesticulate, she is still. Hepburn is the powerful and peaceful eye of a brewing storm. She is at turns loving, brave, sad, proud, and completely deserving of both the adoration she receives and the hostility she engenders in the incorrigible Mary. Only someone as enduringly "pure" (as Karen Wright) could so confound a malicious and desperate schemer.

Mary bullies her vulnerable classmate Rosalie (Veronica Cartwright).

Top: Mary whispers lies about the headmistresses to her grandmother (Fay Bainter). Bottom: Karen, Martha and Joe (Garner) attempt to "clean house" and discover the truth behind the lies.

Despite the unenthusiastic critical response, *The Children's Hour* was nominated for five Academy Awards, including Best Sound, Costume Design, Art Direction, Cinematography, and a nod to Fay Bainter for her supporting role. It was also featured in the 1995 documentary *The Celluloid Closet*, which examines the portrayal of homosexuality throughout Hollywood's history.

Contemporary audiences may find that *The Children's Hour* has acquired new resonance as an allegory for our own preoccupation with gossip and scandal, while young women may find new reasons to idolize Hepburn. The film's final moments belong to her, and she cuts a striking figure: resolute but not hardened, independent but not strident. The picture of beauty and grace.

"Because of the adult nature of its theme — this motion picture is not recommended for children."

– *The Children's Hour* tagline

Opposite page: Karen Wright and Martha Dobie deal with the fallout from the scandal. Top: Shirley Maclaine is both feisty and vulnerable as the troubled Martha. Bottom: A stark figure against a bleak background, Karen contemplates everything that has happened in the film's powerful final scene.

CHARADE (1963)

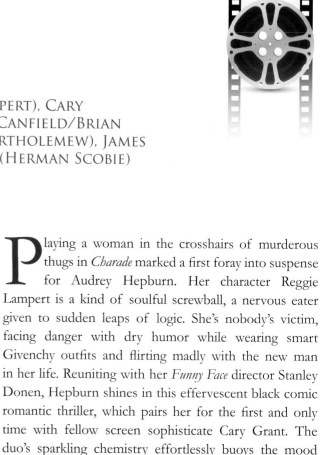

UNIVERSAL PICTURES

DIRECTOR: STANLEY DONEN

SCREENPLAY: PETER STONE

STORY: STONE AND MARC BEHM

PRINCIPAL CAST: AUDREY HEPBURN (REGGIE LAMPERT), CARY GRANT (PETER JOSHUA/ALEXANDER DYLE/ADAM CANFIELD/BRIAN CRUIKSHANK), WALTER MATTHAU (HAMILTON BARTHOLEMEW), JAMES COBURN (TEX PANTHOLLOW), GEORGE KENNEDY (HERMAN SCOBIE) AND LEOPOLD W. GIDEON (NED GLASS)

Playing a woman in the crosshairs of murderous thugs in *Charade* marked a first foray into suspense for Audrey Hepburn. Her character Reggie Lampert is a kind of soulful screwball, a nervous eater given to sudden leaps of logic. She's nobody's victim, facing danger with dry humor while wearing smart Givenchy outfits and flirting madly with the new man in her life. Reuniting with her *Funny Face* director Stanley Donen, Hepburn shines in this effervescent black comic romantic thriller, which pairs her for the first and only time with fellow screen sophisticate Cary Grant. The duo's sparkling chemistry effortlessly buoys the mood even as danger lurks in the glamorous streets of Paris. As violence erupts and the bodies pile up, *Charade* never loses its sense of lighthearted fun.

Unhappily married Reggie first meets dashing Peter Joshua (Grant) at a resort in the French Alps. In a nice bit of foreshadowing, she insists she has no interest in getting

Top: Reggie Lampert (Hepburn) contemplates divorce over lunch. Bottom: Peter Joshua (Cary Grant) returns Jean-Louis Gaudet (Thomas Chelimsky) to his mother Sylvie (Dominique Minot) and introduces himself to Reggie.

further acquainted, telling him, "I already know an awful lot of people. Until one of them dies, I couldn't possibly meet anyone else." In fact, she already is a widow. When she returns to Paris, Reggie discovers that her husband, Charles, has been murdered — and that he was a member of a gang of thieves who stole $250,000 in gold during World War II. Now his co-conspirators — Tex Panthollow (James Coburn), Herman Scobie (George Kennedy), and Leopold W. Gideon (Ned Glass) — are in Paris on the trail of the loot. They and CIA agent Hamilton Bartholemew (Walter Matthau) believe Reggie must at least have *some* idea what happened to it.

Reggie is therefore relieved when Peter appears and quickly becomes her friend, protector and possible lover, all rolled up in one dashing package. "Do you know what's wrong with you? Nothing!" she teases him. It is a belief she cannot quite shake, even when it becomes apparent that Peter's identity is a charade, his name constantly changing along with his back story.

Screenwriter Peter Stone wrote *Charade* with Hepburn and Grant in mind. Then a television writer with a handful of credits, Stone had failed to impress Hollywood executives with his genre-blurring screenplay. Undaunted, he had transformed the script into a novel that the women's magazine *Redbook* serialized as *The Unsuspecting Wife*. Seven Hollywood studios then made offers, but Stone decided to go with Donen, an

Top: Reggie reads her husband's last letter. According to director Stanley Donen and screenwriter Peter Stone, this image is the key to the entire film. Bottom: As Reggie and Sylvie watch in shocked silence, Tex Penthollow (James Coburn) seeks proof that Charles Lampert is really dead.

independent filmmaker with a deal at Columbia Pictures, trusting him to film on location in Paris instead of a Hollywood back lot.

Donen was uniquely positioned to fill Stone's dream cast. *Funny Face*, in which Hepburn plays a bookseller turned model opposite Fred Astaire, had been a triumphant collaboration. The filmmaker also had a close association with Grant, having directed him in *Kiss Them for Me* (1957), *Indiscreet* (1958) and *The Grass Is Greener* (1960). It was Donen who first introduced the actors to one another over dinner in Paris. Grant proved to be a good sport after Hepburn confessed that she was nervous about meeting her idol. He suggested that she put her head down on the table and just breathe. She did, knocking a bottle of red wine onto Grant's tan suit. The incident would inspire Stone to write a scene into *Charade* in which Reggie upends an ice-cream cone on Peter's jacket.

Hepburn was often paired with considerably older leading men, including Astaire in *Funny Face* and Gary Cooper in *Love in the Afternoon* (1957). But the 25-year age difference between him and the 33-year-old actress bothered Grant, who asked

"Even though I wrote this with Audrey in mind, I realized she'd never been in anything like this before. In other words, she had never been in jeopardy. I found her very vulnerable on-screen and vulnerable is what this jeopardy called for."

— Peter Stone, *Charade* screenwriter

Stone for changes in the screenplay, insisting, "I cannot chase the girl. I'm too old. She's too young. I cannot chase this girl. She must in some way be chasing me." It was an inspired suggestion. Hepburn is soft and vulnerable, but she is very much the charming aggressor in a relationship in which the age gap becomes part of the thrust and parry of flirtation. Peter protests when Reggie suggests that he start looking at her as a woman, "I could already be arrested for transporting a minor past the first floor." She is undeterred, sweetly reminding him, "I don't bite, you know, unless it's called for."

Grant still had reservations, leading him to drop out of the movie. Hepburn backed out as well, wanting only to work with Grant. Columbia at first urged Donen to consider recasting the movie with youngsters Warren Beatty and Natalie Wood, but soon dropped the idea and the movie. *Charade* was dead. Then Grant changed his mind and Donen struck a new deal with Universal Pictures. The movie commenced shooting in October 1962.

Charade opened at New York's Radio City Music Hall on December 5, 1963. Reviews were mixed. "First-time teaming of Cary Grant and Audrey Hepburn, a natural, gives the sophisticated romantic caper an international appeal plus the selling points of adventure, suspense and superb comedy," raved *Variety*'s Robert B. Frederick in an early review. The *New York Times*' Bosley Crowther was not so amused, grousing that "this light-hearted picture is full of gruesome violence." Nevertheless, he expressed grudging admiration for Hepburn's performance, writing, "Miss Hepburn is cheerfully committed to a mood of how-nuts-can-you-be."

Opposite page: Hamilton Bartholemew (Walter Matthau) informs the newly widowed Reggie that her murdered husband was a thief. Top: Tex terrifies a trapped Reggie. Bottom: A conspiracy of thieves: Peter confronts Tex, Herman Scobie (George Kennedy), and Leopold Gideon (Ned Glass).

Scobie tries to get his hook into Alexander Dyle (formerly Peter Joshua) on top of the American Express building.

For her performance, Hepburn received a Golden Globe nomination for Best Actress-Musical or Comedy and won a BAFTA award for Best British Actress. Box office were modest, with the film earning just over $6 million, but over the years *Charade* developed a rabid cult following. It inspired a critically lambasted 2002 remake, Jonathan Demme's *The Truth About Charlie,* that left audiences cold, mostly because stars Thandie Newton and Mark Wahlberg couldn't replicate Hepburn and Grant's romantic spark.

Thirty-five years after *Charade*'s release, critic Charles Taylor offered a reassessment of the movie in the online magazine *Salon*. "This is a prankish,

"What do you want me to say, that a pretty girl with an outrageous manner means more to me than a quarter of a million dollars? It's a toss-up, I can tell you that. Hasn't it occurred to you I'm having a hard time keeping my hands off you?"

— Adam Canfield (Grant) to Reggie Lampert (Hepburn)

Top: Reggie and Alex share their first kiss. Bottom: During a romantic walk along the Seine, Reggie spills ice cream on Alex. In real life, Hepburn once spilled red wine on Grant's tan suit.

"Drip dry!" Alex amuses Reggie with an impromptu shower.

playful picture, with a pair of charming jokers at the top of its deck, Grant and Audrey Hepburn," he wrote. "*Charade* still feels fresh, quick-witted, nothing like the artificial, airless Hollywood pictures of its time."

Although *Charade* divided audiences and critics in 1963, Hepburn would make a second, widely praised foray into the suspense genre four years later, when she starred in the nerve-rattling thriller *Wait Until Dark* (1967).

Top: Adam Canfield (aka Peter Joshua/Alexander Dyle) and Reggie come to a new understanding during a Seine boat ride. Bottom: Reggie gets caught in the middle of a climactic showdown between Adam and Mr. Bartholemew at the Palais Royale.

"Even when the imperiled Hepburn lets her nerves get the better of her, she puts quotation marks around her frightened reactions that are as exquisite as a pair of Cartier cuff links."

— Charles Taylor, *Salon.com*

PARIS WHEN IT SIZZLES (1964)

PARAMOUNT PICTURES
DIRECTOR: RICHARD QUINE
SCREENPLAY: GEORGE AXELROD
BASED ON A STORY BY JULIEN DUVIVIER AND HENRI JEANSON
PRINCIPAL CAST: WILLIAM HOLDEN (RICHARD BENSON/RICK), AUDREY HEPBURN (GABRIELLE SIMPSON/GABY), GREGOIRE ASLAN (POLICE INSP. GILET), TONY CURTIS (PHILIPPE THE SECOND POLICEMAN/MAURICE) AND NOEL COWARD (ALEXANDER MEYERHEIM)

A lighthearted remake of the French film *La fête à Henriette* (1952), *Paris When It Sizzles* reunited Audrey Hepburn with William Holden, her co-star from the hit romantic comedy *Sabrina* (1954). As the waifish secretary sent to keep Holden's liquored-up screenwriter in check, Hepburn sparkles amidst the French locales — a winning combination that served her well in a string of hits, including *Funny Face* (1957), *Charade* (1963), *How to Steal a Million* (1966) and *Two for the Road* (1967). Playing the awestruck ingénue, Gaby Simpson, Hepburn imbues the character with all her trademark wit and intelligence, which proves a perfect balance to the more jaded and cynical character of Rick Benson (William Holden).

Lounging about a swanky hotel suite *cum* bachelor pad with the Eiffel Tower looming outside his window, Rick struggles with a case of crippling writer's block. Paid in advance to write a screenplay for Hollywood producer Alexander Meyerheimer (Noel Coward),

Top: Actor/playwright Noel Coward as Hollywood producer Meyerheim. Bottom: Hepburn as Gaby Simpson, dressed to the nines in Givenchy.

Rick has indulged in a bit too much *joie de vivre* and squandered away all his money. With two days left to deliver a script, Rick takes on the spirited and lovely Miss Simpson, whose sheer presence serves as a welcome muse for the infatuated writer. As Rick's imagination takes flight, he begins a series of narratives while a riveted Gaby taps away at the keys. Together they plot out the premise of the screenplay *The Girl Who Stole the Eiffel Tower*. As Rick edits and rewrites the screenplay, these film-within-a-film scenes unfold on-screen, with Fred Astaire, Marlene Dietrich and Frank Sinatra making cameo appearances.

Of note, Holden's voice-over recalls his Oscar-nominated turn as the fallen screenwriter Joe Gillis in *Sunset Boulevard* (1950). In one sequence, Rick launches into a vivid tale of star-crossed lovers with a final act that ends with a cat in a rain-soaked alley as the lovers kiss — a witty nod to the iconic final scene in Hepburn's *Breakfast at Tiffany's* (1961). Similar references to the stars' prior films appear throughout *Paris When It Sizzles;* these reel-life asides perk up the narrative with a tongue-in-cheek artiness that was downright avant-garde by major motion picture standards, circa 1964.

Although Hepburn radiates breezy charm and good humor in *Paris When It Sizzles*, she was initially reluctant to do the film. According to Diana Maychick's *Audrey Hepburn, An Intimate Portrait*, Hepburn only agreed to star in the film after director Richard Quine showed up at her front door with the script, penned by *Breakfast at*

Top: Gaby and Rick (William Holden) brainstorm the absurd storyline for his new screenplay, *The Girl Who Stole the Eiffel Tower*. Bottom: Screen siren Marlene Dietrich makes a cameo appearance in *Paris When It Sizzles*.

Rick tries to drink his way through writer's block.

Tiffany's screenwriter George Axelrod. Recalling their meeting fondly, Hepburn said, "Richard was so sweet. He told me how perfect I'd be for the part. After not feeling so perfect for either of my last two films, his words sounded good. I liked the idea of doing something light, and I liked even more making the decision myself."

At the time, Quine's surprise visit had more to do with tempering a minor complication that might otherwise have dampened his leading lady's spirits — the casting of William Holden as the screenwriter. During the filming of *Sabrina*, Hepburn had fallen madly in love with the married actor. The affair consumed her and spilled over onto the set of *Sabrina*, where the lovers were inseparable, despite the vocal objections of her other leading man, Humphrey Bogart. At the time, Bogart had wanted his wife, actress Lauren Bacall, cast as Sabrina and resented the young starlet for claiming the part. The resulting conflict between the three leads led to an explosive onscreen chemistry that made the film an irresistible box office draw. The affair ended due to Hepburn's desire for a family — something Holden could not provide, due to an irreversible vasectomy.

"It's an action/suspense, uh, romantic melodrama with lots of comedy, of course. And, uh, deep down underneath, a substrata of social comment."

— Rick (Holden)

Fortunately for Quine, Hepburn was eager to reunite with her old flame on-screen: "I was delighted. I didn't show it, but the fact that Bill was in the movie clinched it for me. I hadn't seen him for about ten years. In fact, I think the last time we even said anything to one another was when I introduced him to Mel Ferrer, who was my fiancé at the time, at some nightclub in New York."

Neither Hepburn nor Quine could have predicted the dramatic turn of events that unfolded once filming began on location at the Boulogne-Billancourt Studios in France. Holden, still carrying a torch for the beautiful actress, wound up lost in the bottle in an effort to cope with his heartbreak. Throughout his career, there had been rumors about his drinking, but he'd always kept his bouts with the bottle in check at work. Now, seeing Audrey Hepburn on a daily basis sent him spiraling out of control. The frequency of his stupors sent the budget soaring and nearly led to Paramount shutting down production. To keep the cameras — *and* the studio money — rolling, Quine convinced Tony Curtis to make an extended cameo appearance as a hipster movie star in tight pants who pops up repeatedly throughout *Paris When It Sizzles*.

In addition to Curtis, Mel Ferrer also makes a memorable cameo appearance in the film, but his presence on the set exacerbated, rather than quelled Hepburn's insecurities, much to Quine's dismay. In an atypical display of star temperament, Hepburn demanded that Quine fire cinematographer Claude Renoir after she viewed the first rushes. As she later admitted, "It was as if we all let our worst instincts get

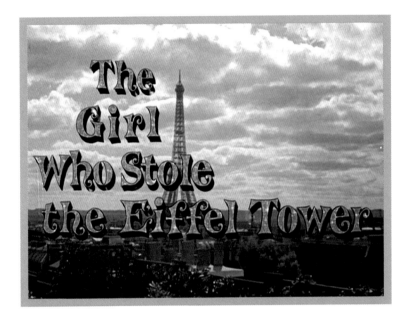

Top: The title credits for the film within the film. Bottom: Tony Curtis contributes a scene-stealing cameo as Maurice, a method actor with "an almost lunatic narcissism!"

the best of us. I realize now I was being manipulative with Bill, that I needed him to pay attention to me to boost my ego. But he was being pathetic, really, and angry, and Richard Quine couldn't control either of us. Though he did try, poor man. He moved next door to Bill's house to keep a lid on his drinking. But it didn't work. Bill would invariably outsmart him and then show up under my window, serenading like a hyena."

Pronounced "a dreadfully expensive display of bad

"...as usual, she brings her extraordinary charm to it, and makes us smile in spite of ourselves, and the ironic picture-within-a-picture plot actually plays better today than it did in the swinging 60's."

– Jeffrey M. Anderson, *Combustible Celluloid*

"That rather grotesque object looming so formidably on the horizon is the Eiffel Tower. I had it moved there to remind me what town I'm in. If it offends you, of course, I'll have it taken away again."

— Rick (Holden)

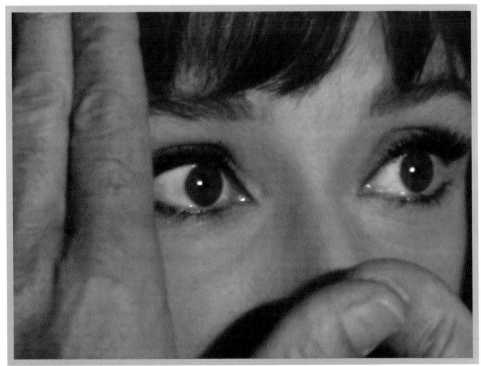

Opposite page: Rick and Gaby in a scene from *The Girl Who Stole the Eiffel Tower*. Top: Gaby attempts to organize Rick's screenplay. Bottom: Hepburn in ravishing close-up.

taste" by Hollis Alpert in *Saturday Review*, *Paris When It Sizzles* fizzled at the box office. Viewed 45 years later, Quine's film now looks inventive and fresh. Admittedly, it's a far from seamless work, yet there's an undeniable vitality to *Paris When It Sizzles* that makes it one of Hepburn's most offbeat and original films.

"Oh! Every morning when I wake up and I see there's a whole new other day, I just go absolutely ape!"

— Gaby (Hepburn)

Opposite page: Hepburn in a scene from *The Girl Who Stole the Eiffel Tower*. Top: Curtis in another fantasy sequence from the film within the film. Bottom: Rick and Gaby celebrate their collaboration.

"Relax, it's all right to laugh at this tender love story!"

— *Paris When It Sizzles* tagline

My Fair Lady (1964)

Warner Bros. Pictures

Director: George Cukor

Screenplay: Alan Jay Lerner

Based on the play by Lerner and Frederick Loewe

Principal Cast: Audrey Hepburn (Eliza Doolittle), Rex Harrison (Professor Henry Higgins), Stanley Holloway (Alfred P. Doolittle), Wilfrid Hyde-White (Colonel Hugh Pickering), Gladys Cooper (Mrs. Higgins), Jeremy Brett (Freddy Eynsford-Hill), Theodore Bikel (Zoltan Karpathy), Mona Washbourne (Mrs. Pearce), Isobel Elsom (Mrs. Eynsford-Hill), John Holland (Butler) and Marni Nixon (Eliza Doolittle [singing voice] [uncredited])

As Eliza Doolittle, the Cockney flower girl transformed into elegant beauty who wins the heart of the irascible linguistics professor Henry Higgins (brilliantly portrayed by Rex Harrison), Audrey Hepburn undertook what was arguably her greatest screen-acting challenge in *My Fair Lady*. Although she had previously danced and sang to fine effect in *Funny Face* (1957), Hepburn lacked the powerhouse vocals for the demanding role, which Julie Andrews had created in the Broadway smash hit musical by librettist/lyricist Alan Jay Lerner and composer Frederick Loewe. But when producer Jack Warner purchased the film rights to *My Fair Lady* for a then-record-breaking sum of $5 million in 1962, he decided to protect his huge financial investment by offering the role to Hepburn, a proven box office draw, instead of the relatively unknown Andrews.

Initially resistant to the idea — she even lobbied Warner studio executives to hire Andrews — Hepburn later accepted Warner's offer when he reportedly began

Top: Eliza Doolittle (Hepburn) sings of life's creature comforts in "Wouldn't It Be Lovely?" Bottom: Eliza takes a bath for the first time.

looking at other actresses to play Eliza. Paid a then-unheard-of salary of $1 million, Hepburn shed her innate elegance to play the Edwardian-era "common ignorant girl" who becomes the pawn in a wager between Higgins and fellow linguist Colonel Hugh Pickering (Wilfred Hyde-White). Contemptuous of Eliza's lower-class cockney accent, Higgins bets Pickering that he can teach the flower girl to speak and comport herself like a society belle in six months.

Both repelled and intrigued by Higgins' offer, Eliza nevertheless swallows her pride to begin weekly elocution and etiquette lessons under this stern taskmaster. After a rocky start, Eliza gradually becomes Higgins' "fair lady" and attracts the interest of society fop Freddy Eynsford-Hill (Jeremy Brett) — much to the dismay of Higgins, who's unexpectedly fallen in love with his protégé.

On stage, Lerner & Lowe's musical adaptation of George Bernard Shaw's *Pygmalion* had made theatrical history, running for 2,717 performances (the longest-running Broadway musical for its time, a record it held onto for nine years). It also won seven Tony Awards (including Best Musical), and great acclaim for its young star Julie Andrews. So when Hepburn, Harrison (reprising his Broadway role after Cary Grant turned it down) and veteran director George Cukor began production on the $17 million budgeted film version in August of 1963, the proverbial bar was set very high, especially for Hepburn.

Top: In a fantasy sequence, Eliza thanks King Charles V of England (Charles E. Fredericks) for proclaiming May 20 as Eliza Doolittle Day. Bottom: Higgins (Rex Harrison), Eliza and Colonel Pickering (Wilfrid Hyde-White) perform "The Rain in Spain."

Eliza savors her moment of triumph.

Fortunately, she brought her decade-long experience working with Hollywood's A-list talent to *My Fair Lady*. Despite her vocal shortcomings, she recorded all the songs — and was led to believe by the studio brass that her vocals would be used in the finished film. However, consummate vocal double Marni Nixon (who had previously dubbed Deborah Kerr's vocals in *The King and I*) ultimately dubbed Hepburn's singing voice on such classic Lerner & Loewe songs as "Wouldn't It Be Loverly?" and "I Could Have Danced All Night."

While Hepburn may not have been up to the musical challenges of the role, she nevertheless forges all her dramatic and comic skills in an immaculate, beautifully realized and superbly crafted performance that grows in stature and resonance upon repeated viewings. Hepburn's willingness to submerge her familiar ethereal screen persona in order to create a poor, lower-class street urchin is particularly striking. Her cockney accent is flawless. Many of her line readings as the flower girl appear improvised and are inspired and fresh, serving to make her transition to fair lady all the more effective. Her appearance on the staircase — elegantly coiffed and magnificently gowned — as she and Higgins depart for the Embassy

"I ain't dirty! I washed my face and hands before I come, I did."

— Eliza Doolittle (Hepburn)

122

Ball is one of those great cinematic moments that leaves one breathless. In the comedy scenes Hepburn's timing is flawless; in the dramatic scenes her instincts note-perfect; and in the musical numbers she appears to be truly in her element — professional, confident and committed, with movements rarely, if ever, betraying her real-life musical and singing limitations.

And what of the film itself? A critical and commercial blockbuster, *My Fair Lady* went on to win eight Academy Awards including Best Picture, Best Actor (Harrison) and Best Director (Cukor), as well as countless other accolades from critics' organizations, the Director's Guild of America and the Golden Globes. Hepburn's performance won high praise, but her name was conspicuously missing from the 1964 list of Best Actress nominees; ironically, the original Eliza, Julie Andrews, won the Oscar that year for her feature film debut, Walt Disney's *Mary Poppins*. Decades later, *Entertainment Weekly* ranked Hepburn's *My Fair Lady* performance as one of the "25 Biggest Oscar Snubs Ever."

One of the last great productions of Hollywood's studio system era, *My Fair Lady* is as close to a work of art as anything produced during that period. It remains to this day a Cinderella-like story, supremely told by a group of professional craftsmen, actors and technicians at the height of their considerable powers. From George Cukor's direction to Alan Jay Lerner's writing; from the superb ensemble cast's performances to Andre Previn's musical scoring; from Cecil Beaton's eye-popping costumes and Gene Allen's superb production design to veteran cinematographer Harry Stradling's photography, *My Fair Lady* is first-rate all the way.

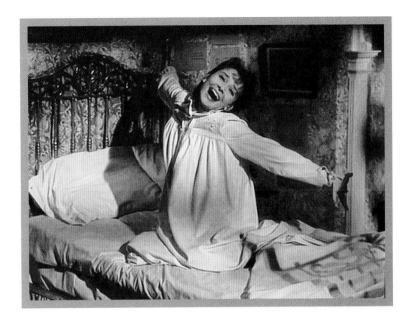

Top: A jubilant Eliza sings "I Could Have Danced All Night." Bottom: Higgins watches as the newly refined Eliza makes small talk with aristocrat Freddy Eynsford-Hill (Jeremy Brett) at Ascot races.

"The part should have been given to Julie Andrews…"

– Hepburn to Barbara Walters on being asked to play Eliza Doolittle on film over Julie Andrews who originated the role on Broadway

Top: "Come on, Dover! Move your bloomin' arse!" Bottom: Pretty in pink: Hepburn in one of Cecil Beaton's Oscar-winning costumes.

124

Eliza's unexpected return.

Director Martin Scorsese once claimed that, although George Cukor was trained in the theater, his films always *looked* like movies. Also, the director's reputation for being exceptionally skilled with actors is on full display in *My Fair Lady*. Rex Harrison's Academy Award–winning portrait of Henry Higgins is essayed with astonishing spontaneity and élan — quite an accomplishment, considering how many times he had previously performed the part on both the Broadway and London stages. The film result is an even deeper and richer performance than on the best-selling Broadway and London cast recordings. Harrison also perfected the talking-on-pitch singing technique for the film

which he had so famously originated on stage, elevating it to an even higher artistic level.

In the end, *My Fair Lady* is quite possibly the finest film version of this material imaginable — a near-perfect film brimming with the theatrical wit, intelligence and poetry of the stage version, and the visual splendor and cinematic qualities that only great filmmaking can provide — augmented, of course, by the majestic screen artistry of Audrey Hepburn.

"Years later I met her (Audrey Hepburn) and she told me 'Oh, Julie, you really *should* have done it, but I didn't have the guts *not* to, which I thought was nice."

— Julie Andrews

"They've made a superlative film from the musical stage show *My Fair Lady* — The happiest single thing about it is that Audrey Hepburn superbly justifies the decision of the producer, Jack L. Warner, to get her to play the title role that Julie Andrews so charmingly and popularly originated on the stage. All things considered, it is the brilliance of Miss Hepburn ... that gives an extra touch of subtle magic and individuality to the film."

— Bosley Crowther, the *New York Times*

Opposite page: One of the stunning sets that won Cecil Beaton the Academy Award for Best Art Decoration. Top: Old friends and rival linguists, Colonel Pickering and Professor Higgins. Bottom: Eliza is greeted as royalty at a sumptuous embassy ball.

How to Steal A Million (1966)

Twentieth Century Fox
Director: William Wyler
Screenwriter: Harry Kurnitz
Story: George Bradshaw
Principal Cast: Audrey Hepburn (Nicole Bonnet), Peter O'Toole (Simon Dermott), Hugh Griffith (Charles Bonnet) and Eli Wallach (Davis Leland)

In *Charade* (1963), Audrey Hepburn played a Parisian widow whose life is endangered by her connection to $250,000 in stolen loot. Three years later, the actress returned to Paris for the frothier, romantic caper spoof *How to Steal a Million*. In Hepburn's third and final film with director William Wyler, the stakes may not be life or death, yet the otherwise lighthearted *How to Steal a Million* is nearly as suspenseful as *Charade*, as a vulnerable beauty risks prison and public humiliation in an attempt to protect her father.

When a Paris art museum asks celebrated art collector Charles Bonnet (Hugh Griffith) to exhibit his Renaissance-era statue the Cellini *Venus*, he's amused to lend out a piece of art he knows is a fake. In contrast, his daughter Nicole (Hepburn) is horrified; her fears seem amply justified when the museum insists on authenticating the piece for insurance purposes. Determined to save her father's reputation and the family's name, Nicole turns to

Top: Nicole Bonnet (Hepburn) enters the picture, motoring down the avenue in her little red roadster. Bottom: An exasperated Nicole confronts her father, Charles (Hugh Griffith), after finding him painting his latest masterpiece.

Simon Dermott (Peter O'Toole), the elegant burglar she recently caught trying to make off with her father's Van Gogh. She proposes a heist, and while Simon cannot understand why she wants to steal her own property, he is smitten enough to agree to her daft plan.

Director William Wyler had never made a caper comedy when Twentieth Century Fox head Richard Zanuck passed Harry Kurnitz's screenplay — then called *Venus Rising* — to him with the promise that he could make the film in Paris. Wyler liked the challenge of trying something new, and the French film industry's habit of starting the workday at noon appealed to him. But as his daughter Catherine revealed in her DVD commentary track for *How to Steal a Million*, the script just didn't excite him, so he hedged his bets, agreeing to make the film only if Hepburn would star. She was his favorite among the actors he directed, and the affection was mutual. After all, Wyler had guided her to a Best Actress Academy Award for her first big role in *Roman Holiday* (1953). And while their second collaboration, *The Children's Hour* (1961), had been a disappointment, Hepburn was "profoundly indebted to him for all of this, because she had hardly been an actress when they first met," according to Catherine Wyler.

Hepburn was also a bigger star than ever thanks to her turn as Eliza Doolittle in 1964's smash hit musical *My Fair Lady*. Despite the closeness of their relationship, Wyler did not believe that Twentieth Century Fox

Top: Nicole frets as M. Bonnet hands over the Cellini *Venus* to museum director Grammont (Fernand Gravey). Bottom: Nicole's first glimpse of burglar Simon Dermott (Peter O'Toole), a man she later describes as "quite good-looking — in a brutal, mean way."

Brash American tycoon David Leland (Eli Wallach) woos Nicole over dinner.

would successfully woo her. But Hepburn, suffering from depression after a recent miscarriage, was eager to get back to the distraction of work.

As it happened the only role in *How to Steal a Million* that was surprisingly difficult to cast was that of Davis Leland, a gauche, wealthy American art collector who woos Nicole in an attempt to secure Cellini's *Venus* for himself. Wyler's first thought was to give the part to Hepburn's *Charade* co-star Walter Matthau, but he demanded $200,000 and equal billing for a small supporting role. Instead, Wyler hired George C. Scott only to fire him after the apparently hung-over actor arrived on the set hours late for his first day of filming, and then left without waiting to talk to his director. Eli Wallach, then starring in the Broadway smash hit comedy *Luv*, took over, so eager to take part in the movie that he agreed to extend his contract with the play by eight weeks to make up for the four weeks he would be otherwise engaged in Paris.

O'Toole a major star since *Lawrence of Arabia* (1962), was far better known for serious drama, having appeared in only one comedy, the slapstick farce *What's*

"She kissed me! I can't get over it — I'm kissing a big movie star and she's so involved in the scene. She's so enchanting that not only do I want the statue, I want her as well."

— Eli Wallach on Hepburn

New Pussycat? (1965), but Wyler thought the 33-year-old Irishman and the still girlish, 36-year-old Hepburn would generate heat together. In fact, what makes the pair so appealing as a screen couple is not heat but humor. *How to Steal a Million*'s plot is inconsequential, the robbery it builds toward nothing more than a cinematic Rube Goldberg device. What makes this bonbon of a movie dazzle is the witty, sophisticated dialogue tossed back and forth by a couple who clearly enjoy each other's company.

Early in the shoot, O'Toole and Hepburn shared close quarters for eleven days — a museum broom closet (!) — so Wyler could film key scenes where Simon and Nicole plot the heist. The two stars spent hours in that cramped space, getting to know each other between takes as Wyler set up his shots. "The whispers and carrying on that went on in that closet!" recalled Catherine Wyler. "They began to break each other up. This then happened throughout the movie. My father said they reacted on each other like laughing gas. Audrey was such an elegant person that you didn't know until you got to know her better how much fun she was."

Wallach shared Wyler's high opinion of Hepburn. He was delighted to meet the actress he had first seen in her Tony Award–winning performance in *Ondine*: "I found her so easy to work with, so involved in the film, so happy to have me [there]." He also found her to be a good sport, willing to let him bend her over backwards for their characters' romantic clinch.

The bonhomie on the set did not translate into big box office or awards for *How to Steal a Million*, although Kurnitz's screenplay received a

Top: Simon and Nicole case the museum from a discreet vantage point. Bottom: "Let's give Givenchy the night off." Simon prepares Nicole's disguise for the robbery.

Writers Guild of America nomination for Best Written American comedy. Critics were split. Pauline Kael wrote dismissively, "The picture isn't offensive, and it's handsome enough, but it's just blah." But Bosley Crowther in the *New York Times* loved it, calling it "a delightful lot of flummery." Whatever the immediate reaction to it was, the movie's breezy charm endures over four decades later, even if it is a little bittersweet: Hepburn would make just two more films, Stanley Donen's *Two for the Road* (1967) and Terence Young's *Wait Until Dark* (1967), before she took a nine-year sabbatical from acting. She would return to the screen in *Robin and Marian* (1976), but *How to Steal a Million* is the last of her truly buoyant comedies.

"You don't think I'd steal something that didn't belong to me, do you?"

— Nicole Bonnet (Hepburn)

"You're at that awkward age: too old to be a juvenile delinquent, too young to be a hardened criminal."

— Simon Dermott (O' Toole) to Nicole Bonnet (Hepburn)

Opposite page: Simon makes off with the Cellini *Venus*. Top: Stuck in a closet, Simon and Nicole give in to their feelings. Bottom: Simon and Nicole rendezvous at the Ritz to celebrate a job well done.

Hepburn and O'Toole spent hours cooped up in a museum broom closet filming this pivotal scene.

"Cheers all around for everybody — for Miss Hepburn, Mr. O'Toole, Mr. Griffith, Eli Wallach, as a wealthy American collector of art, and for the scriptwriter, Harry Kurnitz (who is known fondly as Harry Koverr) and especially for William Wyler, who directed with humor and style."

— Bosley Crowther, the *New York Times*

Top: Scene stealer Hugh Griffith as Charles Bonnet. Bottom: Now what? Nicole and her father brace themselves for disaster.

"You know, for someone who starting lying just recently, you're showing a real flair."

— Simon Dermott (Peter O'Toole) to Nicole Bonnet (Hepburn)

"Having a wonderful crime! Wish you were here!"

— *How to Steal a Million* tagline

Two for the Road (1967)

Twentieth Century Fox

Director: Stanley Donen

Screenplay: Frederic Raphael

Principal Cast: Audrey Hepburn (Joanna Wallace), Albert Finney (Mark Wallace), Eleanor Bron (Cathy Manchester) and William Daniels (Howard Manchester)

As she eased toward an early retirement from motion pictures, Audrey Hepburn chose as one of her final roles a character that would test her range as an actress and surprise the fans who had been so consistently dazzled and delighted by her elegant screen persona. With *Two for the Road* she took on the role of student-turned-socialite Joanna Wallace, and the challenge of portraying a complex character at many stages over a 12-year period. Altering her appearance was part of the process — her hairstyles and clothing help to illustrate the passage of time — but the real challenge for Hepburn was in using body language and voice to convey a change in attitudes, and a gradual shift in her character's feelings about the man she had come to both reject and need.

Two for the Road begins with Joanna and her husband, Mark (Albert Finney), coolly appraising a newlywed couple sitting in stony silence amidst the celebration around them. The newlyweds' expressions mirror the icy détente

Top: Joanna (Hepburn) meets her future husband when she finds his lost passport — in his own bag. Bottom: Joanna applies the elbow grease while Mark (Albert Finney) tends to the clutch.

between Mark and Joanna. Although they seemingly have the outer trappings of success — money, a jazzy sports car, chic clothes — Mark and Joanna can barely speak without sniping at each other. Twelve years after they first met, hitchhiking across the French countryside in the flush of youthful exuberance, the two have hit the road again in France, where they're barraged by memories, both joyous and painful, of prior excursions. From their awkward, vaguely antagonistic first meeting to an idyllic Mediterranean vacation to a nerve-fraying European tour with an "Ugly American" family, *Two for the Road* charts their turbulent, passionate romance. After all the recriminations, betrayals and disappointments, Mark and Joanna worry they've become what they most fear: married people who sits in a restaurant without speaking to each other. But are they still bound by love or just simply bound?

Even in her character's most tragic moments, Hepburn brings a spark to Joanna, who displays cleverness and surprising emotional resilience at every phase in the story; she's consistently in control and impossible to ignore. That's no easy task when acting alongside the charismatic Albert Finney, well-known from his star turn as the lovable rogue in *Tom Jones* (1963), and exhibiting some of the same on-screen appetites for women and food. As the young architect-to-be Mark Wallace, Finney expertly captures the character's arrogance and innocence. At first, he's too full of himself to notice the remarkable young woman

Top: In one of her first screen roles, Jacqueline Bisset plays a flirtatious student who almost derails the Wallaces' budding romance. Bottom: Joanna and Mark become acquainted on a French country road.

Content to be going it alone, Joanna tries her luck at thumbing a ride.

who's decided to give him a chance; in later years, he's too self-absorbed to care. But Mark's crudeness is the catalyst for much of the film's comedy and romantic set-ups, and despite the movie's modern approach, it's this oil-and-water dynamic that keeps *Two for the Road* rooted in the great tradition of classic screen romances like *His Girl Friday* (1940) and *It Happened One Night* (1934).

As the era of the great musicals waned, and a few years before the gritty realism of the early 1970s dominated American cinema, audiences craved mature subject matter — without completely giving up the pleasures of Technicolor splendor, idyllic locations and stars who light up the screen. *Two for the Road* delivered on those counts, and offered up a time capsule of late-1960s cinema, with a Henry Mancini score, the latest in mod fashions, and jump-cuts that chop up the narrative and keep the story surprising from scene to scene. Rather than leading the viewer through the gradual souring of a once-euphoric romance, director Stanley Donen and screenwriter Frederic Raphael intersperse the lowest points of the marriage with the most delightful. They show us a variety of stages, ranging from the unhappy couple's nonstop bickering to the excitement of their first days together, when they

"Just because you use a silencer doesn't mean you're not a sniper."

— Mark Wallace (Finney) to Joanna (Hepburn)

fell in love. With the shifts in narrative, we see them go from poor to wealthy and back again, and see their loyalties shift as well. Most of the action takes place on a multitude of driving trips through the south of France, but the road of their relationship is the point of the film, with plenty of emotional potholes and breakdowns along the way.

The fine supporting cast in *Two for the Road* is headed by Eleanor Bron and William Daniels (also seen on-screen that year in *The Graduate*). They excel as the "Ugly American" couple with an obnoxious child whose road trip with Mark and Joanna ends in comic disaster. A young Jacqueline Bisset, already established from her part in Roman Polanski's *Cul-de-sac* (1966), also makes a notable contribution to the film, if only to show off the sparkle in her eyes that would make her a marquee name in the years to come.

Though she had great faith in Donen, who had previously directed her in *Funny Face* (1957) and *Charade* (1963), Hepburn at first turned down the role of Joanna in *Two for the Road*. The character was starkly different from previous roles — and from her hard-earned public image — and the material, in its more tragic moments, cut too close to the facts of her real-life marriage with actor Mel Ferrer, also in its twelfth year and fading fast. Ferrer saw the part as an opportunity for Hepburn to show how well she could adapt to the new trends in cinema, but he would come to regret that he pushed her into the role, when news of an affair between Hepburn and Finney started to fill gossip pages across the globe. While discreet, the stars themselves would not deny that their mutual admiration had blossomed into a romance.

Top: Mark and Joanna's obnoxious traveling companions on an ill-fated road trip: Cathy and Howard Manchester (Eleanor Bron and William Daniels) with their bratty daughter Ruthie (Gabrielle Middleton). Bottom: Mark and Joanna rough it in the great outdoors.

"I didn't even know the Audrey of the last few weeks on this film," Donen later recalled. "She overwhelmed me. She was so free, so happy." But her mood changed drastically in the final days of shooting, after Ferrer confronted her about the affair, and Hepburn became deeply concerned about how the situation might affect her 6-year-old son, Sean. The romance with Finney ended abruptly, but the joy and disappointment she poured into her character lives on in *Two for the Road*.

Although it received an Academy Award nomination for Best Original Screenplay, *Two for the Road* was not an immediate hit with either critics or audiences. Over the years, however, a cult following developed around the film,

"If there's one thing I really despise, it's an indispensable woman."

— Mark Wallace (Finney) to Joanna (Hepburn)

Opposite page: Joanna and Mark escape the rain in a concrete pipe. Top: On the French Riviera, the infatuated couple bliss out on sand and sunshine. Bottom: Bitter but beautiful, the Wallaces make the mod party scene.

which is now regarded as one of the most thoughtful and nuanced American films about marriage.

For Hepburn, *Two for the Road* ultimately stands as a bittersweet triumph. Despite the toll it took on her marriage, the film contains what Donen regards as "her best performance."

"They'll never be anyone else like you in my life."

— Joanna Wallace (Hepburn)

"You haven't been happy since the day we met, have you? If only you were 10 years younger and you knew what you know now."

— Joanna Wallace (Hepburn) to Mark Wallace (Finney)

Opposite page: A happy moment behind the wheel. Top: Love hurts: the sunburned couple attempt to make love. Bottom: Mark and Joanna revel in each other's company. Her marriage to Mel Ferrer dissolving, Hepburn fell into an affair with Finney while shooting *Two for the Road*.

WAIT UNTIL DARK (1967)

WARNER BROTHERS-SEVEN ARTS

DIRECTOR: TERENCE YOUNG

SCREENPLAY: ROBERT AND JANE-HOWARD CARRINGTON

BASED ON THE PLAY BY FREDERICK KNOTT

PRINCIPAL CAST: AUDREY HEPBURN (SUSY HENDRIX), ALAN ARKIN (ROAT), RICHARD CRENNA (MIKE TALMAN), JACK WESTON (CARLINO), JULIE HERROD (GLORIA) AND EFREM ZIMBALIST JR. (SAM)

At a time when Hollywood was scrambling to lure the "youth market" into theaters, Audrey Hepburn proved that old-fashioned star power still filled seats with the box office hit *Wait Until Dark*. The back-to-basics style of Terence Young's thriller — filmed almost entirely on one set, with a small ensemble cast — proved to be just what audiences wanted, as Hepburn bid a temporary farewell to her film career.

Hepburn's innate warmth and vulnerability heightens the emotional impact of her performance in *Wait Until Dark*. As Susy Hendrix, a woman recently blinded in an accident, she portrays a character literally lost in darkness and anxious about managing on her own. Living with her photographer husband Sam (Efrem Zimbalist Jr.) in a brownstone walk-down apartment in New York City, she worries about crime in the neighborhood, despite Sam's assurances that she's safe at home when he's off on a

Top: Mike Talman (Richard Crenna) and Carlino (Jack Weston) listen as their ringleader Roat (Alan Arkin) explains his plan to retrieve the doll and its valuable contents. Bottom: Susy Hendrix (Hepburn) senses she is not alone in her apartment.

photo shoot. But then Sam inadvertently brings danger right to their door, when he unknowingly accepts a doll stuffed with heroin from a woman in the airport. A trio of criminals soon descends on the couple's apartment to retrieve the contraband by any means necessary. With Sam away, they con their way into the apartment with an elaborate ruse — posing as an old army buddy, a police detective and an old man — but as Susy becomes wise to the deception, the criminals ramp up their aggression, forcing her to rely on her wits to survive.

Unfolding over the course of one evening in Susy's apartment, *Wait Until Dark* effectively ratchets up the tension with the arrival of the criminals' psychotic ringleader, Roat (Alan Arkin). Originally written for the stage by Frederick Knott (who also wrote the stage play *Dial M for Murder*), the action is confined almost entirely to one room in the Hendrixs' apartment, adding the same powerful element of claustrophobia that Alfred Hitchcock employed to unnerving effect in his psychological thrillers *Lifeboat* (1944), *Rope* (1948) and *Rear Window* (1954). In fact, Hepburn had turned down a Hitchcock role in 1959 (in the never-produced *No Bail for the Judge*) because she objected to the character's helplessness in the face of a violent attack. In *Wait Until Dark*, Hepburn imbues Susy Hendrix with a tenacity and wit that evens the playing field and gives her character a fighting chance, despite her physical impairment.

To portray the film's blind heroine convincingly, Hepburn studied with the Lighthouse Institute for the

Top: Roat shows the gloves he uses to avoid leaving fingerprints at the scene of a crime. Bottom: In the relative safety of a sunny afternoon, Susy chats with a neighbor outside her St. Luke's Place apartment.

Lured away on false pretenses, Sam Hendrix (Efrem Zimbalist Jr.) assures Susy she'll be safe alone in their apartment.

Blind and learned to read Braille. According to director Terence Young, then best known for bringing 007 to the screen, the star quickly learned "to find her way, blindfolded.... She mastered the routine of filling a kettle, lighting the gas, boiling the water, putting tea in a teapot and pouring it without spilling a drop."

Audiences loved *Wait Until Dark*, which grossed nearly $11 million for Warner Bros. Pictures. For her stirring performance Hepburn received Golden Globe and Academy Award nominations for Best Actress in a Leading Role. Critics lauded the film, including Bosley Crowther of the *New York Times,* who gave Hepburn full credit for the film's appeal: "The sweetness with which Miss Hepburn plays the poignant role, the quickness with which she changes and the skill with which she manifests terror attract sympathy and anxiety to her and give her genuine solidity in the final scenes."

In contrast, the actors playing *Wait Until Dark*'s trio of criminals are less convincing. Then a relative newcomer, Arkin had previously established himself as a comic actor with his Academy Award–nominated performance in the farce

"Do I have to be the world's champion blind lady?"

— Susy Hendrix (Hepburn) to Sam Hendrix (Zimbalist Jr.)

The Russians Are Coming, The Russians Are Coming
(1966), so it's a bit of a stretch to accept him as a
psychotic thug. The same can be said for veteran
character actor Jack Weston, then probably best
known for his appearances on the television
sitcom *Bewitched*, as Roat's accomplice Carlino.
And Richard Crenna, familiar to audiences as
the helpful teen Walter Denton in the 1950s TV
series *Our Miss Brooks*, comes across as far more
friendly than sinister as Mike Talman, even after
his true intentions are revealed. Efrem Zimbalist
Jr. fares better in his small role as Sam Hendrix,
and teenaged actress Julie Herrod, reprising her
stage role as Susy's precocious neighbor Gloria,
holds her own opposite Hepburn.

Wait Until Dark was produced by Hepburn's
husband, Mel Ferrer, who compounded their
marital difficulties with his controlling hand
on the set, and by assuming duties normally
handled by Hepburn's manager and agent.
Hepburn enjoyed a much happier rapport with
director Terence Young, whom she had met
more than two decades earlier; as a teenager,
she had volunteered in a Dutch medical clinic
where Young, a British paratrooper, was
recuperating from injuries suffered in the the
Battle of Arnhem. Their paths had crossed
again in 1950, when Young had interviewed
the novice actress for a role in his film, *Valley
of the Eagles*. Although he had rejected her
for the role, Young knew then that Hepburn
was destined for stardom: "I hoped one day
she would remember me and get *me* to direct."
Together, Young and Hepburn brought a bit
of British culture to the set when each day,
at precisely four o'clock, they called for a tea
break with the entire production team.

Top: With help from her young neighbor Gloria (Julie Herrod), Susy
learns that her visitors are not who they claim to be. Bottom: Susy
realizes her life is in danger.

When shooting was complete, Ferrer stayed behind at Warner Bros. studios to oversee editing of the picture while Hepburn returned to Switzerland to be with her 6-year-old son and resume a stable life in the family's farmhouse. Though only 38 years old, Hepburn was ready to retire from motion pictures. "I really quit when my son Sean became of age to go to school," Hepburn explained simply. "I could not bear to be separated from him, so I stopped working."

Hepburn would not appear in another film for nine years — and accepted only four more film roles over the next 22 years — effectively removing herself

"No, honey, they're not detectives. They're sure not detectives."

— Susy Hendrix (Hepburn) to Gloria (Herrod)

Opposite page: Surrounded
by the thugs, Susy becomes
a prisoner in her own home.
Top: Susy discovers the phone
line has been cut. Bottom:
Susy attempts to turn the
tables on Roat.

from the industry that had brought her international fame and adulation, as well as marital discord and intense public scrutiny. But with *Wait Until Dark,* she made an elegant, albeit temporary exit, giving film lovers a thrilling, original performance that would continue to excite new audiences long after she had taken her bow and walked away.

A blind woman plays a deadly game of survival!

— *Wait Until Dark* tagline

Opposite page: The terrifying climax of *Wait Until Dark*. Top: Hepburn learned Braille and studied at a school for the blind to prepare for her role in *Wait Until Dark*. Bottom: Roat toys with his captive.

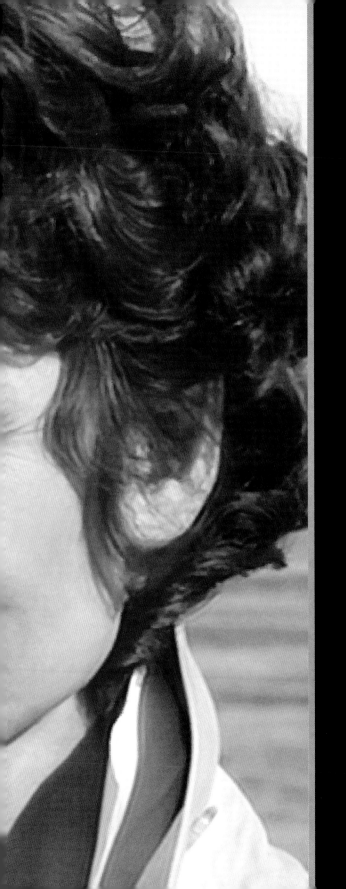

PART 4

1976-1989

AUDREY HEPBURN: 1976-1989

Director Terence Young, who had worked with Hepburn on *Wait Until Dark* (1967), described what it took for Hepburn to accept a film role in the 1970s:

"You spend a year or so convincing her to accept … that she might make another movie…. Then you have to persuade her to read a script. Then you have to make her understand that it is a good script. Then you have to persuade her that she will not be totally destroying her son's life by spending six or eight weeks on a film set. After that, if you are really lucky, she might start talking about costumes. More probably she'll say she has to get back to her family … but thank you for thinking of her."

In 1968, Hepburn met and married psychiatrist Andrea Dotti, and subsequently divided her time between her estate in Switzerland and Dotti's home in Rome, Italy. In 1970, she gave birth to her second son, Luca. Though she would flatly deny in later interviews that she retired from acting, she had, in fact, left the industry for what was, ostensibly, domestic bliss. She returned to the film world only occasionally to appear in the Academy Award ceremonies, or in charitable projects like 1971's *A World of Love*, a TV documentary highlighting the work of UNICEF around the world.

> "I adore cooking and love to garden. Dull, isn't it?"
>
> — Hepburn

In an interview with *Vogue* magazine, she said, "Today there are so many [things], and the more there is, the less I want." She disliked Hollywood's infatuation with graphic sex and violence. Also, she felt she was too old for most of the roles by which younger actresses like Jane Fonda, Faye Dunaway and Mia Farrow were making their names. By the time she was offered the title role in *Robin and Marian* (1976), she had not made a movie in nine years. The studio system that had shaped her career and her image was gone. But the role of Marian represented two things she valued: romance and maturity.

The near financial collapse of most of Hollywood's major studios in the late 1960s had paved the way for the corporate takeovers and mergers of the 1970s. Studio moguls were replaced by corporate accountants and strategists, most of whom lacked the filmmaking savvy — and sincere passion for films — of their predecessors. A film was more likely to be greenlit according to marketing data than by the quality of the script. Thanks largely to film school graduates like Steven Spielberg and George Lucas, the 1970s also saw the creation of a new monster that would need to be fed: the summer blockbuster. Big-budget genre films — and their sequels — flooded theaters throughout the late '70s and '80s. The 1980s box office, especially, would be driven by testosterone-fueled action flicks and violent war films like *Die Hard* (1985) and *Platoon* (1986). The youth market saw more teen-centered popcorn fare ranging from John Hughes' *Sixteen Candles* (1984) and *Ferris Bueller's Day Off* (1986) to raunchy sex romps like *Porky's* (1982). Perhaps rightly so, Hepburn surmised there was no longer a place for the kind of films she liked to make.

Nor did Dotti push her to work like Ferrer had during their 14 year marriage. So Hepburn perhaps felt freer to select — and reject — projects based solely on her own judgment and whims. Most notably, she turned down the role of the tsarina in *Nicholas and Alexandra* (1971), and of the divorcee in *Forty Carats* (1973), the latter because the studio rejected her request to shoot in Rome. Later on, because it stirred too many of her own wartime memories, she rejected what became Liv Ullman's role in the World War II film *A Bridge Too Far* (1977).

She was, however, interested in Anne Bancroft's part in *The Turning Point* (1977), largely because it would allow her to draw from her own background in dance. But Bancroft had already agreed to the part before Hepburn was even apprised of it. Hepburn had also agreed to a biopic about the life of writer Karen Blixen (Isak Dinesen), provided that Fred Zinnemann (*The Nun's Story*) directed. The deal was nearly sealed, but Hepburn's agent Kurt Frings nixed it, assuming his client would never again do another picture. Sydney Pollack would later direct Meryl Streep in the role of Isak Dinesen in the Academy Award–winning *Out of Africa (1985).*

Despite her dedication to her family, however, Hepburn would find her second marriage dissolving. In 1981, she met actor Robert Wolders, who had recently lost his wife, actress Merle Oberon. In 1982, her divorce from Dotti became final, and even though, or perhaps *because* they never married, Hepburn and Wolders remained together for the duration. He was the gentle spirit Hepburn needed. He had no wish to dominate her. He simply made her happy.

HEPBURN'S LEADING MEN, 1976-1989

SEAN CONNERY
Robin and Marian (1976)

Firmly putting 007 behind him, Connery plays a weary, broken-down Robin Hood to Hepburn's middle-aged Marian in Richard Lester's revisionist historical romance. The Scottish superstar earned some of the finest reviews of his career for *Robin and Marian*, which ranks as one of Connery's best films of the 1970s, along with *The Man Who Would Be King*
(1975) and *The Wind and the Lion* (1975)

RICHARD DREYFUSS
Always (1989)

The Oscar-winning actor was in the midst of a late-1980s career renaissance when he shared the screen with Hepburn in *Always* (1989). The sentimental romantic fantasy is the third film Dreyfuss made with director Steven Spielberg; the others were *Jaws* (1976) and *Close Encounters of the Third Kind* (1977). Dreyfuss won the 1977 Best Actor Academy Award for *The Goodbye Girl* (1977)

BEN GAZZARA
Bloodline (1979)

Best known for his starring roles in *Anatomy of a Murder* (1959) and several John Cassavetes films, the veteran Broadway actor enjoyed a brief but passionate affair with Hepburn during the filming of *Bloodline*, the critically panned adaptation of Sidney Sheldon's bestseller. Gazzara would rebound later that year in Peter Bogdanovich's well-received character study, *Saint Jack* (1979).

ROBIN AND MARIAN (1976)

COLUMBIA PICTURES

DIRECTOR: RICHARD LESTER

SCREENPLAY: JAMES GOLDMAN

PRINCIPAL CAST: SEAN CONNERY (ROBIN HOOD), AUDREY HEPBURN (LADY MARIAN), ROBERT SHAW (SHERIFF OF NOTTINGHAM), NICOL WILLIAMSON (LITTLE JOHN) AND RICHARD HARRIS (KING RICHARD THE LIONHEART)

Audrey Hepburn's return to the silver screen after a nine-year hiatus was more than an unexpected pleasure for her countless fans. Her performance in *Robin and Marian* was a triumphant comeback that affirmed yet again her unrivaled beauty, grace and dignity. The movie remains a delight, crammed with pleasures large and small. A poignant blend of action, romance, offhand comedy and bittersweet nostalgia that imagines the reunion between Maid Marian and Robin Hood some 20 years after their impassioned youthful courtship, *Robin and Marian* is one of those movies that grows deeper and richer as the years go by — and, not coincidentally, as the viewer progresses through life's stages.

Hepburn had turned down several high-profile roles during her self-imposed retirement before James Goldman's unusually compassionate and intelligent script captured her interest. Sean Connery had already

Top: Little John (Nicol Williamson) and Robin Hood (Sean Connery) ponder the imminent consequences of defying King Richard the Lionheart. Bottom: The mortally wounded King Richard the Lionheart (Richard Harris) berates Robin Hood for his perceived betrayal.

signed on, and Hepburn's sons — keen to meet the actor they'd idolized as James Bond — lobbied their mother to accept the part. As an added enticement, the film was scheduled to be shot in Spain, in part to accommodate a few of the cast's big-name actors who avoided England and its tax policies. That suited Hepburn, who lived in Rome, for it allowed her children to join her on location.

Of course, it was the role that attracted Hepburn above all other considerations. She'd always had an impeccable instinct for recognizing which parts played to her strengths versus which were absurd or unflattering. The grown-up Marian, standing for virtue and tenderness amid the brutality of medieval England, was a perfect fit. "Everything I'd been offered in recent years had been too kinky, too violent or too young," she said. "I had been playing ingénues since the early 1950s, and I thought it would be wonderful to play somebody of my own age in something romantic and lovely."

Given his pick of projects after the critical and commercial success of *The Three Musketeers* (1973) and its 1975 sequel, director Richard Lester reportedly agreed to direct *Robin and Marian* based on a one-sentence pitch: "Robin Hood as an old man meets Maid Marian." Initially, Lester and the film's producers wanted Hepburn's *Two for the Road* co-star Albert Finney to play Robin, with Connery as his sidekick Little John. Thankfully, that idea went nowhere, for Finney lacks the

Top: Robin Hood's great love Marian (Hepburn), who's lived in a convent for 20-odd years. Bottom: Age did not diminish Hepburn's extraordinary beauty; she was 47 years old when she made *Robin and Marian*.

larger-than-life stature the role requires; it's impossible to imagine anyone besides Connery playing an aging yet still vital Robin Hood.

For all his recent success with British period pieces, Lester was an unexpected choice to direct an old-fashioned film with a sensitive heart and middle-aged characters. He had made his name with the frenetic Beatles films *A Hard Day's Night* (1964) and *Help!* (1965), and the antiwar black comedy *How I Won the War* (1967). Lester had also come out of television and still adhered the small screen's accelerated shooting schedule, which initially put him at odds with Hepburn, who was used to working at a much more leisurely pace. It took a bit of time for Hepburn to adjust, but neither her discomfort nor Lester's manner can be discerned in the finished film. *Robin and Marian* displays an unexpected classicism and restraint for Lester, and a gently rhythmic pace that suits both the story and the characters.

The powers that be made one other impeccable call. Goldman, who had won an Academy Award for *The Lion in Winter* (1968), originally called his new script *The Death of Robin Hood*. This downbeat title aptly evoked the loss of

The peace-loving Marian rebuffs Robin's aggressive offer to help her evade the Sheriff of Nottingham.

"For Robin and Marian, love is the greatest adventure of all."

— *Robin and Marian* theatrical trailer

idealism and rise of cynicism that defined the post-Watergate, post-Vietnam era, but would have meant death where it counted most — at the box office. The title *Robin and Marian*, on the other hand, gave the yarn a romantic spin while also signaling to moviegoers that Hepburn, whose entrance doesn't occur until nearly half an hour into the picture, was nonetheless a central figure in the story.

Robin and Marian, of course, trades on the immortal love story that leavened *The Adventures of Robin Hood* (1938), starring Errol Flynn as the virile bandit who steals from the rich and gives to Sherwood Forest's poor, and Olivia de Havilland as King Richard the Lionheart's beautiful and spirited ward. Michael Curtiz's Technicolor feast, a standout Warner Bros. entertainment, endures as an ebullient and rollicking swashbuckler for all ages.

Goldman and Lester pick up the tale some 20 years later, with the passion and innocence of young love tempered by years of battle and solitude, as well as by the natural aging process. Robin has been off wreaking havoc in distant lands alongside King Richard the Lionheart (Richard Harris) on the disastrous Crusades, and hasn't seen England in two decades. No longer a maid, Marian has lived in a convent since her lover declared himself more loyal to his sovereign than to her.

Robin and Marian begins in France, amid the tawdry and bizarre final act of Richard's military folly. When the loyal Robin defies an unjust order, King Richard tosses him and Little John (Nicol Williamson) in a cell in preparation for their execution. But fate spares the men, and

Top: Marian snaps the reins on the getaway wagon after Robin Hood and Little John free the nuns from the Sheriff's control. Bottom: Robin and Marian, sans wimple for the first time, rekindle old affections after the day's adventures.

they head home in peace to Sherwood Forest, where the Sheriff of Nottingham (Robert Shaw, evoking happy memories of the last time he tangled with Connery, in the 1963 Bond film *From Russia With Love*) is waiting, ready to do the new king's bidding and renew his rivalry with Robin.

The heart of the film, though, is the renewal of acquaintances between Robin and Marian. "I was right to love you all those years ago," he announces. "It's odd," she replies thoughtfully, "I know I loved you but I can't remember how it felt, or who I was." Like all men, Robin assumes that he and Marian can just pick up where they left off, a bit wiser, a bit sadder, but just as devoted to each other as they were in the old days.

"Robin Hood as an old man meets Maid Marian."

— screenwriter James Goldman's original one-line premise

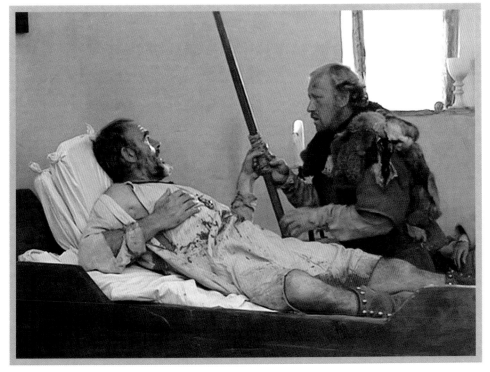

Opposite page: Connery and Hepburn make an inspired team in *Robin and Marian*. Top: Little John and Marian watch helplessly while Robin fights the climactic battle. Bottom: A warrior to the end, Robin asks Little John for his bow.

Marian realizes it's a fantasy, however, for Robin has lived by the sword for so long that the soldier's code is all he knows. She sees his character more clearly than he sees hers, and tries to explain it to him. "I'll do everything for you but mourn," she declares, and while we get her meaning, Robin resists it. *Robin and Marian* isn't about the cost of war so much as the cost of being a warrior.

Reviewers were split on the film's merits — *Chicago Sun-Times* critic Roger Ebert echoed the reservations of many when he took Lester and Goldman to task for the film's uneven blend of broad comedy and pathos — yet they all welcomed Hepburn's long-awaited return to the screen. As *Time*'s Jay Cocks put it, "We are reminded of how long it has been since an actress has so beguiled us and captured our imagination."

Erasing the gulf between a medieval nun and the modern woman she embodied throughout the 1950s and 1960s Hepburn does a beautiful job of playing a period heroine. Both she and Connery generate gentle comedy out of growing older (seven years before the Scotsman simultaneously mocked and embraced the idea of an aging action hero in his Bond reprise *Never Say Never Again*), while acknowledging that sexual desire does not vanish at 40. That's just one of the reasons that the adult-oriented *Robin and Marian* wears better with every passing year that Hollywood abandons mature topics and themes in shameless pursuit of the youth market. Best of all, *Robin and Marian* gives us the timeless Hepburn in her last great role — poised and possessed, steadfastly pointing the way toward kindness, and civilization.

"Everything I'd been offered in recent years had been too kinky, too violent or too young. I had been playing ingénues since the early 1950s, and I thought it would be wonderful to play somebody of my own age in something romantic and lovely."

— Hepburn

Top: As expressive as ever: Hepburn in the film's heartbreaking final scene. Bottom: A hero's final act.

BLOODLINE (1979)

PARAMOUNT PICTURES

DIRECTOR: TERENCE YOUNG

SCREENPLAY: LAIRD KOENIG

BASED ON THE NOVEL BY SIDNEY SHELDON

PRINCIPAL CAST: AUDREY HEPBURN (ELIZABETH ROFFE), BEN GAZZARA (RHYS WILLIAMS), JAMES MASON (SIR ALEC NICHOLS), CLAUDIA MORI (DONATELLA), IRENE PAPAS (SIMONETTA PALAZZI), MICHELLE PHILLIPS (VIVIAN NICHOLS), MAURICE RONET (CHARLES MARTIN), ROMY SCHNEIDER (HELENE ROFFE-MARTIN), OMAR SHARIF (IVO PALAZZI), BEATRICE STRAIGHT (KATE ERLING) AND GERT FROBE (INSPECTOR MAX HORNUNG)

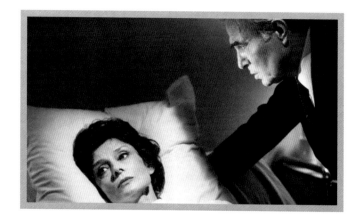

On paper, *Bloodline* seemingly had all the ingredients for a juicily entertaining popcorn flick — one of those glossy, all-star productions that Hollywood used to crank out with assembly-line regularity during its studio system heyday. Yet despite the presence of Audrey Hepburn and an international cast of screen luminaries, Terence Young's adaptation of Sidney Sheldon's bestselling 1977 novel was greeted by a chorus of boos from critics and audiences alike. In bringing Sheldon's page-turning blend of kinky sex, murder and corporate intrigue to the screen, Young and screenwriter Laird Koenig somehow drained the narrative of coherence, momentum and suspense. But while it's incontestably the worst film of Hepburn's career, *Bloodline* is not quite as irredeemably awful as its dire reputation suggests.

Taking a role turned down by Candice Bergen, Jacqueline Bisset and Diane Keaton, Hepburn stars as Elizabeth Roffe, the beautiful paleontologist daughter

Top: Sir Alec Nichols (James Mason) tries to console Elizabeth (Hepburn) in the hospital. Bottom: Twenty years after they worked together on *The Nun's Story*, Beatrice Straight and Hepburn reunited to co-star in *Bloodline*.

of the head of a global pharmaceutical empire. When her father dies mysteriously in a mountain-climbing accident, Elizabeth reluctantly assumes the burden of running Roffe Pharmaceuticals — and confronting the company's board of directors, comprised of her cousins Sir Alec Nichols (James Mason), Simonetta Palazzi (Irene Papas) and Helene Roffe-Martin (Romy Schneider), among others. Citing her inexperience, they immediately ask Elizabeth to step down and let them take Roffe Pharmaceuticals public; otherwise, the debt-ridden, lawsuit-plagued global entity will surely perish. Overwhelmed but defiant, Elizabeth vows to keep the global entity a family business.

Deadly complications ensue, however, when an Inspector Hornung (Gert Frobe) arrives on the scene to inform Elizabeth that her father was murdered, most likely by someone in his inner circle. All the evidence points to her cousins, each of whom stood to gain financially if the company were sold. The only person Elizabeth can seemingly trust is Rhys Williams (Ben Gazzara), her late father's chief assistant, or so she thinks. Meanwhile, a string of murders involving the pornographic film industry appear to be linked to Roffe Pharmaceuticals. As the body count rises, Elizabeth races to find the murderer to save the company and herself.

The first R-rated film of Hepburn's career, *Bloodline* marked her return to the screen after a three-year break. Why she chose to star in this unabashed potboiler mystified critics and longtime fans. For Hepburn, the

Top: Elizabeth with Rhys Williams (Ben Gazzara), the one man she *hopes* she can trust. Bottom: Elizabeth barely escapes with her life.

lure was partly financial; she needed the money to support her family, especially since her second marriage to Italian psychiatrist Andrea Dotti was ending. Dotti's liaisons with other women were becoming gossip column fodder, much to Hepburn's embarrassment. At the end of her tether, she gave him an ultimatum: If he didn't stop carrying on with other women in public, she'd have no choice but to go back to work. When Dotti refused, Hepburn agreed to star in *Bloodline* for her old friend Young, who had previously directed her to an Academy Award nomination in *Wait Until Dark* (1967). That *Bloodline* would be filmed relatively close to Hepburn's home in Italy also appealed to the star, who didn't want to be separated from her sons.

Hepburn's affair with co-star Gazzara was a welcome distraction from the unhappy experience of shooting *Bloodline*.

Unfortunately, the production of *Bloodline* was beset by problems from the beginning. Coordinating the international location shooting in Copenhagen, London, Munich, New York, Paris, Sardinia and Sicily proved difficult for Young, as did wrangling some of Hepburn's co-stars. At one point, Irene Papas claimed that she had forgotten how to act. James Mason got so frustrated with the delays and script problems that he shouted, "I can't take any more of this!"

As for Hepburn, she soon came to regret her decision to make *Bloodline,* particularly after she became aware of the sleazy elements in Koenig's screenplay; her requests for changes fell on deaf ears. A passionate affair with co-star Gazzara proved momentarily diverting, but for the most part, Hepburn was anxious and chain smoking during the production. In fact, while traveling with her bodyguards to film a scene in Sicily, she remarked that it would be better to be kidnapped by the Mafia than have to finish the picture. It was later revealed that *Bloodline*'s European and American investors had used the production as a tax shelter, so quality filmmaking was probably never their primary focus.

Critics unanimously savaged *Bloodline,* which Roger Ebert branded "reprehensible" in his *Chicago Sun-Times* review. The *New York Times'* Vincent Canby complained that "*Bloodline* takes Miss Hepburn's Givenchy clothes more seriously than it does the actress who wears them." Canby didn't even bother to review the film's performances. The only one who truly emerged unscathed from the debacle was novelist Sheldon, who had pocketed $2 million for the film rights and was "laughing all the way to the remedial writing class," according to Ebert.

Audiences shared critics' derision for the film, which flopped at the box office. But even Canby begrudgingly admitted that *Bloodline* had "a more attractive, more able cast" than the previous film version of a Sheldon novel, *The Other Side of Midnight* (1977). It also boasts sumptuous cinematography by Freddie Young and a lilting score by Ennio Morricone. Granted, Young makes some odd directorial choices that don't pay off, the narrative is murkily drawn and the performances, even from the normally reliable Mason and Academy Award winner Beatrice Straight (who co-starred in *The Nun's Story*) are inconsistent. (The odd post-dubbing and sound mixing quality doesn't help.)

Although she was reportedly devastated by the film's poor critical and commercial reception, Hepburn nimbly rises above the debacle of *Bloodline* by sheer virtue of her innate elegance and dignity. Then on the cusp of 50, she may be a bit too old to play the film's 35-year-old heroine convincingly, but she nevertheless looks ravishing in her Givenchy clothes and Bulgari jewels.

Hepburn's fans hoped that *Bloodline* would not prove to be their idol's cinematic swan song. Happily for them, Hepburn was not finished with films just yet.

"No matter how friendly the fox, never let him in your hen house. Sooner or later, foxes get hungry."

— Elizabeth Roffe (Hepburn)

THEY ALL LAUGHED (1981)

TIME-LIFE FILMS/TWENTIETH CENTURY FOX

DIRECTOR: PETER BOGDANOVICH

SCREENPLAY: PETER BOGDANOVICH

PRINCIPAL CAST: AUDREY HEPBURN (ANGELA NIOTES), BEN GAZZARA (JOHN RUSSO), JOHN RITTER (CHARLES RUTLEDGE), COLLEEN CAMP (CHRISTY MILLER), PATTI HANSEN (SAM THE TAXI DRIVER), DOROTHY STRATTEN (DOLORES MARTIN), GEORGE MORFORGEN (MR. LEONDOPOULOS), BLAINE NOVAK (ARTHUR BRODSKY), SEAN FERRER (JOSE) AND GLENN SCARPELLI (MICHAEL NIOTES)

After the critical and commercial failure of *Bloodline* (1979), Audrey Hepburn would take her final starring role in a Hollywood film that would turn out to be the complete antithesis of *Bloodline*, both in terms of content and budget: Peter Bogdanovich's offbeat, shot-on-the-fly romantic comedy *They All Laughed*. Playing an Italian industrialist's unhappy wife — a role written expressly for her — Hepburn brings old-style Hollywood glamour and grace to a film that's developed a cult following since its truncated release.

A meandering, seriocomic valentine to the glories of New York and beautiful women, *They All Laughed* follows the exploits of three private detectives who specialize in trailing spouses suspected of infidelity. Cool, calm and collected John Russo (Ben Gazzara) is assigned to pursue and track Angela Niotes (Audrey Hepburn), who's come to Manhattan in search of adventure. Meanwhile,

Top: Angela Niotes (Hepburn) in search of Manhattan adventure. Bottom: Pursued by private detectives Arthur Brodsky (Blaine Novak) and John Russo (Ben Gazzara) Angela and her son, Michael (Glenn Scarpelli), duck into the FAO Schwartz toy store for target practice.

his partners Charles Rutledge (John Ritter) and Arthur Brodsky (Blaine Novak) take the enviable job of shadowing Dolores Martin (Dorothy Stratten), the scintillatingly beautiful young wife of a jealous husband. As the three detectives trail Niotes and Martin through the streets and bars of New York, surprising bonds are forged and love blooms in Bogdanovich's loosely structured and bittersweet narrative.

In the early 1970s, Bogdanovich had been a Hollywood "golden boy," thanks to such acclaimed films as *The Last Picture Show* (1971), *What's Up Doc?* (1972) and *Paper Moon* (1973). By 1980, however, he was widely considered a has-been whose spiraling ego had gotten the better of his filmmaking talents, most notably in the case of the box office and critical flop musical *At Long Last Love* (1975). In 1979, he had somewhat redeemed himself with the low-budget character study *Saint Jack*, starring Ben Gazzara as a Singapore brothel owner, but the major studios no longer regarded Bogdanovich in the same league as Francis Ford Coppola, his former partner in the short-lived Directors Company.

Determined to make a comeback, Bogdanovich began working on *They All Laughed* and flew Hepburn to Los Angeles in 1980 to discuss her role in what was then an unfinished screenplay. He would eventually base the character of Angela Niotes on elements of Hepburn's own life, in particular her love affair with Ben Gazzara (with whom she became intimately involved while the two were making *Bloodline)*. Her salary would be $1 million for six weeks' work, plus a sizable account

Top: Angela suddenly realizes she's being followed.
Bottom: Hepburn at her most beguiling.

for expenses. And, perhaps to ensure her participation, Bogdanovich would hire Hepburn's son Sean Ferrer to be his personal assistant and play a small role in the film.

In fact, Bogdanovich would ultimately base his entire script on the personalities and real-life experiences of all of the actors. The result is an original and inventive ensemble film that's smart, unsentimental and energetic, with observant and oblique dialogue that zings and crackles. *They All Laughed* is firmly rooted in the director's passion for women (including his deep admiration for Hepburn), who are at its center. Along with Hepburn and Stratten — the ill-fated Playboy model who became Bogdanovich's fiancée — *They All Laughed* features Colleen Camp and model Patti Hansen in eye-catching supporting roles. As Bogdanovich explained, the film's theme and focus is the "immediate, visceral, sexual connection" between men and women.

Shot during the spring and summer of 1980, with cameras often positioned many blocks away from the actors, *They All Laughed* features Hepburn wearing copies of the clothes she wore in real life — blue jeans, silk shirts, pea coat and sunglasses — and puffing away on cigarettes (she was reportedly a three-pack-a-day smoker). All of the actors, including Hepburn, would wait in the city shops

"Now you know why my husband has me followed. I'm a brazen woman who cannot be trusted."

"Some of them promised they'd never fall in love"

— *They All Laughed* tagline

between takes until they were needed in front of the camera, and only 10 extras were used on the busy Manhattan streets (to mask other cameras used during filming). All of the people in the street scenes are real people going about their business in the city.

The brutal murder of Stratten by her estranged husband just weeks after shooting wrapped cast a pall over *They All Laughed*. Twentieth Century Fox let it gather dust on the release shelf until Bogdanovich invested $5 million of his own money to get it into theaters. Ignored by audiences, *They All Laughed* divided critics; whereas *Variety* hailed it as "Bogdanovich's best film to date," the *New York Times'* Vincent Canby called it "an immodest disaster … aggressive in its ineptitude." As for Hepburn, Canby wrote "Mr. Bogdanovich treats [Hepburn] so shabbily that if this were a marriage instead of a movie, she'd have grounds for immediate divorce."

In the face of such scathing reviews, Bogdanovich's quirky film quickly disappeared from theaters (the director himself subsequently filed for bankruptcy). Yet over time, *They All Laughed* has been discovered and embraced by a new generation of filmmakers, such as Wes Anderson (*Rushmore*), who regards it as "a beautiful film." And in a 2002 *Sight and Sound* poll of directors, Quentin Tarantino voted *They All Laughed* the sixth best film of all time!

Although Hepburn receives top billing in *They All Laughed*, she is the not the "star" per se, but a member of the ensemble cast. For all its flaws, Bogdanovich's film is noteworthy for its honest and moving portrait of Hepburn at 52 — still beautiful and regal, with a trace of sadness for what has passed, and a power and a poignancy that still resonates.

Top: Art imitates life: Ben Gazzara and Audrey Hepburn playing roles based on their own real-life love affair. Bottom: A wistful parting: private eye Arthur Brodsky says goodbye to Angela and her son, Michael.

ALWAYS (1989)

UNIVERSAL PICTURES

DIRECTOR: STEVEN SPIELBERG

SCREENPLAY: JERRY BELSON AND DIANE THOMAS

PRINCIPAL CAST: RICHARD DREYFUSS (PETE SANDICH), HOLLY HUNTER (DORINDA DURSTON), BRAD JOHNSON (TED BAKER), JOHN GOODMAN (AL YACKEY) AND AUDREY HEPBURN (HAP)

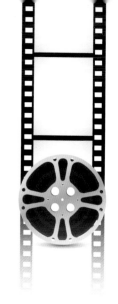

Few would have guessed that Audrey Hepburn would make her final film for the king of the box office blockbuster, Steven Spielberg. Indeed, it was initially hard to picture the ultrarefined Hepburn appearing in one of Spielberg's escapist, special effects–fueled crowd pleasers. But the Hollywood icon revered for her elegance and grace brought her extraordinary career to a close with a role many felt she was born to play: an angelic being in *Always*, Spielberg's loose remake of *A Guy Named Joe* (1943).

As a boy, Spielberg had been deeply moved by *A Guy Named Joe*, Victor Fleming's sentimental film about a dead bomber pilot (Spencer Tracy) returning to Earth to mentor an upstart (Van Johnson) and bid farewell to his grieving fiancée (Irene Dunne). After establishing himself as Hollywood's most bankable director with *Jaws* (1976) and *Close Encounters of the Third Kind* (1977), Spielberg turned his attention to remaking *A Guy Named Joe*. In fact, he wrote a script in 1980, but put it aside to work on other

Top: "Hello, Pete." Hap (Hepburn) welcomes Pete to the great hereafter. Bottom: Hap readies Pete (Richard Dreyfuss) for his ghostly return.

films. As he explained in a 1989 interview, "I wasn't ready to make it…. If I had made it in 1980, I think it would have been more of a comedy. I'd have hidden all of the deep feelings."

Years later, in the wake of a painful divorce from his first wife, Amy Irving, Spielberg returned to the film that had gripped his imagination since childhood. Working with veteran screenwriter Jerry Belson (*Smile*), Spielberg jettisoned the original film's World War II setting to set *Always* in the contemporary American West, where daredevil firefighter pilot Pete Sandich (Richard Dreyfuss) perishes on what was supposed to be his final mission. Awakening in a heavenly way station, Pete meets the angelic being Hap (Hepburn), who dispatches Pete back to Earth to take care of unfinished business. Not only will Pete serve as a guardian angel to a new firefighting pilot, Ted Baker (Brad Johnson), but he will also watch over his fiancée Dorinda (Holly Hunter) to ensure that she makes a new life without him.

In casting Dreyfuss and Hunter as *Always'* romantic leads, Spielberg wanted "real people that we could relate to," versus glamorous Hollywood stars. Dreyfuss, who reportedly shared Spielberg's affection for *A Guy Named Joe* — they quoted the film throughout the making of *Jaws* (1976), according to Roger Ebert — brings his scruffy, everyman quality to Pete. Fresh from the success of *Broadcast News* (1987), Hunter makes Dorinda a down-to-earth and no-nonsense heroine.

In contrast to Dreyfuss and Hunter, Hepburn brings an unmistakable touch of old Hollywood elegance to

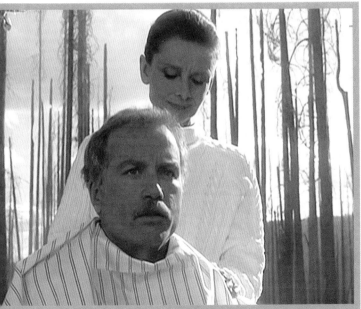

Top: Perfect casting: Hepburn as an angelic being.
Bottom: Cocky no more: Pete finally realizes he's dead.

her extended cameo as Hap, a role Spielberg first offered to Sean Connery. Dressed all in white, she cuts a luminous figure as Pete's otherworldly guide who may or may not be an angel. As Hepburn admitted, "Nobody knows what I am, not even Steven Spielberg. I would say I'm a spirit." Although she's on-screen for just over seven minutes, Hepburn makes the very most of her brief screen time. Speaking in a near whisper, she radiates gentleness and quiet strength in her two scenes with Dreyfuss.

For many critics, Hepburn's brief return to the screen after an eight-year absence is the unmistakable highlight of *Always,* which opened to mixed reviews and tepid box office.

Despite its spectacular, firefighting set pieces, uniformly fine performances and a handful of genuinely touching moments, *Always* never coheres into an emotionally satisfying film. Spielberg's cinematic bravura overwhelms the narrative, which veers uneasily between teary sentiment and broad humor. Nor is there a sense of genuine dramatic urgency to *Always,* no matter how hard Spielberg tries to ratchet up the tension in the firefighting scenes. As Ebert wrote in his *Chicago Sun-Times* review

Dreyfuss and Hepburn: two Academy Award winners.

"Either I'm crazy or I'm dead."

"You're not crazy, Pete."

— Pete Sandich (Dreyfuss) with Hap (Hepburn)

of Spielberg's passion project, "The result is a curiosity: a remake that wasn't remade enough."

But if critics were cool towards *Always,* they were elated to see Hepburn onscreen one last time. In his otherwise dismissive review of Spielberg's film, *Rolling Stone* critic Peter Travers hailed Hepburn as "incandescent" and praised "her movie-star magic." In her cinematic swan song, the 60-year-old Hepburn proved to be the greatest special effect of all in *Always.*

"Audrey Hepburn is incandescent … movie star magic … effortless grace that shows why she is still a legend."

— Peter Travers, *Rolling Stone*

Top: Hepburn received $1 million for six weeks of work on *Always.*
Bottom: Holly Hunter as Dorinda, Pete's fiancée and fellow pilot.

FILMOGRAPHY

Dutch in Seven Lessons (1948)

One Wild Oat (1951)

Laughter in Paradise (1951)

Young Wives' Tale (1951)

The Lavender Hill Mob (1951)

Secret People (1952)

Monte Carlo Baby (1952)

Roman Holiday (1953)

Sabrina (1954)

War and Peace (1956)

Funny Face (1957)

Love in the Afternoon (1957)

Green Mansions (1959)

The Nun's Story (1959)

The Unforgiven (1960)

Breakfast at Tiffany's (1961)

The Children's Hour (1962)

Charade (1963)

Paris When It Sizzles (1964)

My Fair Lady (1964)

How to Steal a Million (1966)

Two for the Road (1967)

Wait Until Dark (1967)

Robin and Marian (1976)

Bloodline (1979)

They All Laughed (1981)

Always (1989)